By Berton Rouéché

Black Weather

The Greener Grass

The Last Enemy

Eleven Blue Men
and Other Narratives of Medical Detection

The Incurable Wound
and Further Narratives of Medical Detection

The Delectable Mountains
and Other Narratives

The Delectable Mountains

AND OTHER NARRATIVES

The Delectable Mountains

AND OTHER NARRATIVES

by

Berton Roueché

Little, Brown and Company · *Boston* · *Toronto*

PS 3535
R89d

The pieces that comprise this book
were written between 1946 and 1953,
and first appeared in the *New Yorker*.
They are reprinted here in substantially
their original form.

*Published simultaneously in Canada
by Little, Brown & Company (Canada) Limited*

PRINTED IN THE UNITED STATES OF AMERICA

To
Bradford Roueché

How vainly men themselves amaze
To win the Palm, the Oak, or Bays,
And their uncessant Labours see
Crown'd from some single Herb or Tree,
Whose short and narrow vergèd Shade
Does prudently their Toils upbraid;
While all Flow'rs and all Trees do close
To weave the Garlands of repose.

Andrew Marvell: THE GARDEN

Contents

The Delectable Mountains

AND OTHER NARRATIVES

The Steeple

ONE early autumn afternoon, on a day of wild winds and sudden silences, I drove out to the village of Sag Harbor to make a pilgrimage to the Whalers' Presbyterian Church there. Sag Harbor is on the north shore of the southeastern fluke of Long Island and covers a secluded point on Shelter Island Sound, near the head of Gardiners Bay. It was settled around the beginning of the eighteenth century. For a few years just before the Revolution, it was a busier port than New York; it once had as rich and restless a whaling fleet as New Bedford or Nantucket; it has been almost motionless since the Civil War; and it is full of big, splendid, creaky old houses and intimations of mortality. The Whalers' Church, although little more than a hundred years old, is its noblest and most disquieting structure. It would be arresting anywhere. Except for a mean and slovenly copy in Essex, Connecticut, it is the only building of its kind in the world.

The Whalers' Church was designed by Minard Lafever, a gifted and expensive New York architect, whose more accessible works include the Church of St. James, near Chatham Square, and the Church of the Holy

Trinity, in Brooklyn, and it was put together by local shipbuilders and ships' carpenters. The foundation was laid in the spring of 1843 and the church was dedicated on May 16, 1844. It cost seventeen thousand dollars. That was an immense sum in the eighteen-forties (carpenters were paid a dollar and a half for a twelve-hour day, the finest St. Croix rum sold for three cents a glass, and clear Havana stogies were two cents each), but it was not considered excessive by Sag Harbor Presbyterians. Most of the parishioners who made substantial contributions to the building fund were whaling officers, shipyard owners, shipowners, or ship chandlers and outfitters, and several were among the wealthiest men on Long Island; practically all the members of the congregation, including farmers and shopkeepers, held rewarding shares in at least one whaler. The first Sag Harbor whaling voyage on record was made in 1775, by a brig called the *Lucy*; she returned home with some three hundred barrels of oil on that occasion. The last Sag Harbor whaler was the *Myra*; she put out in July, 1871, and never returned.

In the intervening years, Sag Harbor whalers made more than five hundred successful voyages, many of which lasted three or four years, and brought back between twenty-five and thirty million dollars' worth of whale oil, sperm oil, and whalebone. The first ship to sail through the Bering Strait was the *Superior*, a Sag Harbor whaler, in 1848. The first American ship to enter a Japanese port was the *Manhattan*, in 1845, commanded by Mercator Cooper, a Sag Harbor whaling captain; Commodore Matthew C. Perry, who is commonly celebrated for this feat, turned up off Japan eight years later. Between 1820 and 1850, Sag Harbor's richest period, the local fleet brought in a total of 83,102 barrels of sperm oil, 812,595 barrels of whale oil, and 6,728,809 pounds of bone, with an aggregate value of more than fifteen million dollars. The industry began to decline in the eighteen-fifties, and it collapsed in the sixties; an abundance of petroleum, which had just been discovered in western Pennsylvania, had all but put an end to the demand for whale oil. The Whalers' Church was completed in Sag Harbor's most vigorous year; the town's fleet in 1844 numbered sixty-three vessels, and its population was 3621. Sag Harbor no longer has even the semblance of a fleet, its harbor is deserted except for a few pleasure craft in summer, its railroad station has been boarded up since 1939, and its population 2373.

Sag Harbor is surrounded on the north and east by the waters of Shelter Island Sound, and a sandy cove hems it in on the west. Above it, to the south, rises a wilderness of scrub oak and jack pine that stretches almost to the ocean, seven miles away. Three or four rambling, humpbacked roads, cut through the woods, link the village to the Montauk Highway, which skirts the seacoast. On the day of my visit I turned into one of these roads at about two o'clock. After a couple of miles, I passed a woman on a wobbly bicycle. Farther on, I passed a weathered sign: "Good Luck and Safe Return — Welcome to Sag Harbor." Just beyond it was a cemetery. Then the road curved, and I emerged abruptly into a wide, angular, downhill street of arching elms and peeling white clapboard houses. The houses sat close to the sidewalk, behind rickety picket fences; there were leaded fanlights over most of their doorways, and one had a widow's walk on the roof. An elderly man in a blue serge suit and an Army sweater was puttering around in one of the yards. He was the only human being in sight. I pulled up and asked him if he could direct me to the Whalers' Church. He leaned on the fence and gazed at me.

"Want to have a look at it, eh?" he said. "Well, it's a sight. Should have come down here ten years ago, though, before the hurricane carried off the steeple. Wouldn't of been any need to ask your way then. You'd of seen it for yourself from here, downstreet, or anywhere. Far as that goes, you could see it from Montauk. That steeple was two hundred feet high, more or less, and there wasn't two parts of it alike. They were every one different. That steeple really tickled me. I enjoyed looking at it. Religion aside, of course. I run with the Methodists, when I go." The old man fished a package of chewing gum from his pocket, popped a stick into his mouth, and jerked his thumb in the direction I was headed. "Two blocks down, turn left at the blinker, and you'll see it," he said. "I guess there's enough of it left to hold you."

I thanked him and drove on down the windy, deserted street. The air smelled wet and salty. As I made the turn at the blinker, a ragged army of gulls wheeled overhead. Then I saw the church. It came hulking up through the heaving treetops — big and baleful and as white as an old clamshell. Set on a wooded knoll, well back from the street, between a row of splayed early-eighteenth-century cottages and a crumbling graveyard, it looked larger than Grand Central Station, and it held me. I parked my car and got out and stared at it. It is a numbing blend of the chaste, the finical, and the stolid. Its façade is predominantly Babylonian and Theban Egyptian in style. The auditorium — of clapboard, slate-roofed, boxy, and severe — is pure meeting-house Colonial. A kind of annex, jutting out in back, is mid-Victorian. From where I stood, at one end of a semicircular walk leading up to the church, only a corner of the main body of the building was visible. The auditorium is a hundred and thirty feet long, sixty-five feet wide, and the equivalent of three considerable stories in height, but the façade obscured it. A massive, shingle-sided, hundred-foot truncated pyramidal wooden tower, some forty feet square at the base and tapering to almost half that at the top, forms the center of the façade. It is flanked by two similar, though broader and slightly lower, wing pylons. Surmounting each of the pylons and the tower is a fragile parapet. The cornices are decorated with a complicated Corinthian frosting. A toothy row of antefixes conceals the eaves. Just below this is a banding of classic-Grecian verticals. An uncovered porch, with an iron-pipe railing, runs the width of the façade. Opening onto it are three narrow, story-high, white, paneled doors, one in the tower and one in each pylon. The antefixes are repeated on their cornices, and the center door is crowned by another parapet. Above each door, and rising almost to the roof line, is a tall window of opaque and faintly lavender small-paned glass. I stood there for a minute or two gazing up at the church, and then I started up the walk leading to the porch. It was hard to imagine a mighty steeple rearing above that vast, chalky face. The building didn't look at all incomplete. It didn't even look old. It looked like a brand-new mausoleum.

I tried all three doors and found them locked. As I turned uncertainly away from the last one, I heard voices approaching, and then a sudden shriek of laughter. I almost jumped. Then an unshaven old man in work clothes and a hunting cap came around the side of the building. With him was a somewhat younger woman. She had on a pink dress, a grass-green coat, and golden slippers, and there was a red patent-leather pocketbook under her arm. I went over to them. They were laughing and chattering, but they broke off when they saw me, and stopped dead. I said I had come out from New

York to see the church and asked if the pastor was around.

"Here?" the man said, studying me closely. "Ain't he down to the Manse?"

His companion giggled. "If Reverend Crawford was here," she said, "he'd have me down on my knees. He's been praying for me to find a job. I'm praying right along with him, too."

"He's down to the Manse," the man said. "Either that or he's out preaching a funeral."

"Probably a funeral," the woman said cheerfully. "There's nothing likelier in this town. How many did you say he had last week, Mr. Cleveland?"

"Four," Mr. Cleveland said. "I doubt there's one to-day, though."

The woman turned to me. "Mr. Cleveland, here, is sexton of the church," she said. "He knows everything that's going on. That's why I come by and see him— to learn the news."

"Sexton, janitor, superintendent, and a little bit of everything else," Mr. Cleveland said. "You might say I've got more jobs here than there is congregation. We had eighty turn up last Sunday. There's room in there for a thousand, spread out just four to the pew. I guess they used to fill her up — sides, center, and gallery — but not in my time. Nor in my dad's, neither. In the old days, most everybody in town was Presbyterian. The R.C.s got the edge now."

"I wonder why that is," the woman said. "Unless it's those Poles and Italians at the watch factory."

"Times change," Mr. Cleveland said. "I remember when there was steamboats running down to New York from here and over to New London, and Sag Harbor was the end of the main line of the Long Island Railroad. That was in the nineties, before they built on out to Montauk and stuck us off on a branch. Now we ain't even on that. You must of drove out here — you don't look like you walked. Well, I've got the time and the right to open her up and let you in — done it before for visitors. But maybe you'd better get Crawford to take you through. Since you come all the way out from New York, he'd be sorry to miss you. You see that gray house with a fence around it down there at the end of the block — where that old dog is laying in the drive? That's the Manse. I'll show you one thing, though. You've heard about the famous steeple we had, I guess, and how it went down in the hurricane. September 21, 1938, at three-thirty in the afternoon, was the date. Well, see that patch of new-looking concrete in the walk there, alongside the burying-ground wall? That's where the butt of the steeple hit. I live just the other side of the burying ground, and I was looking out the window and I saw it go. I couldn't hardly believe my eyes. Why, that steeple had been there all my life. What happened was the wind caught under the louvers in the Sir Christopher Wren section. It lifted the whole shebang straight up in the air — the whole hundred and fifty-or-more feet of it — swung it clear of the building, and dropped it on the walk there. Then it toppled over into the burying ground and smashed to smithereens. All except the bell. That didn't get a scratch on it. We've got it set up inside now, in the lobby. I won't say I heard the bell ring because I didn't. I was inside, and the wind was too loud. But I know people that did. It rang once, hanging up there in midair, just before it hit. And that patch there is the exact spot where the steeple come down."

"I've got a piece of it at home for a souvenir," the woman said. "I guess everybody in town has. Mine's part of the Chinese part."

I left Mr. Cleveland and his friend on the church steps and walked down to the Manse. The sidewalk tilted every which way, and there were tree roots as big as my arm pushing up through the cracks. Most of the houses in the block were so old that moss was growing on their roofs. The dog in the driveway made a half-hearted attempt to rise as I pushed through the front gate, and then slumped somnolently back. Before I could knock at the door, it swung open and a sleek, bald, broad-shouldered man of about forty looked out. He wore metal-rimmed glasses and had on a red flannel shirt, faded dungarees, and dirty white sneakers, and he was eating an apple. "Heard you at the gate," he said, a bit indistinctly. Then he swallowed, grinned, and added, "It's as good as a bell." I introduced myself and explained why I was there. "That's fine," he said. "I'm Donald Crawford. Excuse me." He tossed the core of his apple over my head, out into the street. "Come right in. You picked a good day for your visit. For me, anyway. This is my day off — hence these clothes. I've been burning some trash." I stepped into a dim hall. From upstairs came the sound of running water and an occasional wail. "That's my little helper," Mr. Crawford remarked. "Douglas, aged four. He's enduring a bath. Our other treasure is at school. Mary Alice is seven. Let's go in the parlor." I followed him into a small, high-ceilinged room gently ravaged by time and children. A tall, lanky, white-haired man in a somber suit and a high collar was leaning against the mantel of a handsome white marble fireplace. In an ash tray at his elbow lay an elaborate spiral of apple peel. "This is Dr. Charles H. Tillinghast," Mr. Crawford said to me. He hasn't got a care in the world. He's just retired after forty-nine years of dentistry, and he recently ended a long term as president of our church board of trustees. You're not interrupting anything. He just dropped by for a chat. How about it, Doctor? Would you like to go up to the church with us?"

Dr. Tillinghast extended me a bony hand. "My boy," he said, "it would be a privilege to show you through. Historic Sag Harbor and its proudest monument, the Whalers' Church, are the chief interests of my declining years. As you may know, we have here the second-largest number of authentic Colonial buildings of any community in the United States. We are exceeded only by Nantucket. But even Nantucket, if I may say so, has no such church as ours. My one regret is that our glorious steeple is gone. You've read of it, I'm sure. Perhaps you have seen pictures of it. A work of art." He shook his head. "It was the crowning glory of Minard Lafever's ecclesiastical masterpiece. I miss it as I would an old and cherished friend."

"I'll go get my coat," Mr. Crawford said.

Dr. Tillinghast nodded, cleared his throat, and continued, "It was a loss that everyone felt deeply. One of our local poetesses, the late Annie Cooper Boyd, wrote very movingly about it. I believe I have a copy of her poem here. You might care to glance at it." He drew a wallet from his pocket, extracted a tousled clipping, and handed it to me. The poem, eleven stanzas long, was entitled "The Steeple." It began:

> The Steeple — what! — the Steeple —
> Don't say that *it* has gone!"
> Thus spoke the village people
> With voice and face forlorn.

Another stanza read:

> Oh, lovely, lofty steeple,
> We loved thee from the heart —
> Thy curious construction,
> Thy myriad types of art!

"Of course," said Dr. Tillinghast as I returned the clipping, "we must be thankful that the church itself was spared."

Mr. Crawford, wearing an elegant covert-cloth top-coat, appeared in the hall doorway. I helped Dr. Tillinghast into his coat, he placed a floppy hat on his head, and we filed out to the street. Just outside the gate, Dr. Tillinghast halted. "Perhaps," he said, "we should call our young friend's attention to some of the historic points of interest adjacent to this particular corner. The magnificent Greek Revival edifice that you have undoubtedly noticed directly across the street is the old Benjamin Huntting place. Its architect was none other than Minard Lafever. I see that surprises you. I'll admit that the resemblance between Sag Harbor's two examples of the great Lafever's art is not pronounced. The answer lies in the fact that he was a man of great versatility. Captain Huntting was one of our whaling princes and, I'm proud to say, a prominent member of our church. In fact, like myself, he served as president of our board of trustees. His home was built in 1846. It was later purchased by Mrs. Russell Sage, whom we claim as a fellow-citizen and esteem as a generous civic benefactor."

"She put a new coat of paint on the church once," Mr. Crawford said.

"At least once," Dr. Tillinghast said. "Including the steeple. The old Huntting place is now our Whaling Museum. That large white clapboard structure over there on the right is the old Hannibal French mansion, built around 1800. And behind those trees in the distance is the old Customs House, built in 1790. In its yard is a boxwood bush that there is every reason to believe was grown from a slip presented to our first Collector of Port by Martha Washington herself. Our port, unfortunately, was discontinued in 1905, but the old Customs House, quite properly, has been preserved."

"Don't forget the Manse, Doctor," Mr. Crawford said. He grinned at me and began to move on up the street. "Built in eighteen-twenty-something and never restored. It's a good thing I'm handy."

"I know, Donald," Dr. Tillinghast said mildly. "As I recall, Mr. Barrett often said the same."

"My predecessor," Mr. Crawford explained. "I'm Number Nineteen in the line. The ministry here goes back to 1794. It gives me a funny feeling sometimes to realize that this church had already gone through four generations of ministers before my home town was even founded."

"You're not from around here?" I asked.

"Hardly," Mr. Crawford said. "I'm from Chicago — Winnetka, to be exact. If you'll forgive me, Doctor, I'm not sure that I'd ever even heard of Sag Harbor until I received my call. That was only back in 1940. I must say it seems like a lifetime ago, though. Time sags along pretty slowly in Sag Harbor."

Dr. Tillinghast smiled a thin smile. "The name of Sag Harbor, as Donald knows, does not refer to that, however," he said. "It derives from a Shinnecock Indian word, *sagaponack,* which means 'place of the ground-nuts.' Groundnuts are an edible root, something like a potato."

"Actually," Mr. Crawford said, "my call to Sag Harbor wasn't much more unexpected than my call to the ministry. My mother has never really got over that. Selling stocks and bonds was more the custom in our family. I may not look it, but I used to be a bond salesman. As soon as I got out of Yale — I was class of '28 — I went right into a brokerage house back home. Sold bonds all day and danced all night. Then the market crashed. That did something to me. It wasn't simply a matter of economics. I can't explain it — I walked around in a daze. Then, one Sunday night in November, 1929, I wandered into the old Moody Church, on North LaSalle Street. That evening changed my entire life. I came out converted. I went on selling bonds, of course. I had to. But I spent my nights at the Moody Bible Institute, studying the Bible and making up for lost time. When I was ready — in 1936 — I quit my job and came East and started all over again, at Princeton Theological Seminary. My family — well, one of my aunts — helped put me through. I was ordained in 1940. That was an eventful year for me. I was ordained, I got married, and I got this call. My wife is a Philadelphian. We were on our honeymoon when the call came, and she cried for hours." He shrugged. "She likes it here now — we both do. Sag Harbor's a little off the beaten trail, but there's a tremendous spiritual challenge here. When a whole town lives in the past . . . I mean there are some extraordinary problems."

"Youth is always restless," Dr. Tillinghast said comfortably. He turned to me. "It might interest you to know that the Long Island *Herald*, founded in Sag Harbor in 1791, was the first newspaper published on Long Island. No one would have called this off the beaten path a hundred years ago. One of America's greatest preachers, Edward Hopper, served our church from 1852 to 1863, and it was the daring seamen of Sag Harbor who inspired him to write his immortal hymn 'Jesus, Saviour, Pilot Me.' James Fenimore Cooper lived here for some years, before he established himself as a writer. *The Pioneers* and *The Sea Lions* are both full of Sag Harbor. Why, this very street has known the tread of half the races of mankind. It was nothing in the old days to see Fiji Islanders, Malayans, Kanakas, Chinamen, Portuguese, Shinnecocks, and Montauks, and heaven only knows what else, roaming all over town. I imagine you've read *Moby Dick*. Old Melville knew what he was doing when he had his pagan harpooner Queequeg brought to America on a Sag Harbor whaler."

"Well," Mr. Crawford said, with a wave of his hand, "there she blows — the church that whale oil built. I sometimes think that God placed me in Sag Harbor to humble me, but He certainly gave me a beautiful church."

The sight of the church was momentarily silencing. Familarity didn't seem to diminish it. Even Dr. Tillinghast gazed at it without comment. There was no sign of Mr. Cleveland or his friend. Nobody spoke until we were halfway up the walk. Then Dr. Tillinghast gave a short puzzled laugh. "In all fairness," he said, "I should point out that our church has attracted a few — a very few — unfavorable criticisms. We had an architect visiting here one summer who called it a hodgepodge. The unconventionality of its parts apparently blinded him to the beauty of the whole. He was from one of the newer settlements in the Middle West."

I remarked that Lafever must have been an extremely imaginative man.

"Lafever scorned the commonplace," Dr. Tillinghast said. "The old Benjamin Huntting place, though traditional, has many unusual touches. But I'm not sure that the style of our church was entirely Lafever's idea. His was the guiding hand, of course, but it must be remembered that he was dealing here with men who sailed the Seven Seas and had absorbed the flavor of foreign lands. They had their own ideas. What Lafever did was combine their impressions with his own. I think he was also inspired to suggest something of their courageous way of life. Look at the curious design of the railings up there on the tower and the pylons and over the center door. One of our less appreciative visitors said they looked like a row of lollipops." A trace of pain crossed Dr. Tillinghast's face. "Of course," he went on, "that motif is a stylized version, in what I take to be the Gothic manner, of the whaler's blubber spade. That would be obvious to anyone who had examined the fine collection of old Sag Harbor whaling implements at the Museum. Ridicule comes easy to some people. It may surprise you to hear that even our steeple was not completely immune to criticism. The Sag Harbor *Corrector,* now defunct, once called it 'fantastic' and Lafever 'bewildered.' If you could only have seen that glorious steeple! Perhaps I can describe it to you. It rose, naturally, from the top of the tower, and the height of it was truly majestic — one hundred and eighty-seven feet. Its height was another seafaring note. Our mariners wanted their church spire to serve as a landmark, visible to the returning ship as it rounded Montauk Point. For many years, a whale-oil beacon lamp at the pinnacle was lighted every night."

"I've read somewhere that it used to be noted on the U.S. Coast and Geodetic Survey maps," Mr. Crawford said.

"Very likely," Dr. Tillinghast said. "Our steeple was composed in three tapering sections, each smaller in diameter than the one beneath it. I don't think it was accidental that it resembled somewhat the sea captain's spyglass in use at that time. I doubt, too, if anyone but a shipwright could have raised it. It was raised by ox power, each section pulled up through the inside of the preceding one. The lowest section, in which the bell was installed, was in the seventeenth-century English style of Sir Christopher Wren, and extremely decorative. The main feature of it was an octagonal colonnade. In its pediment were four beautiful clocks. The derivation of the second section is uncertain. It was probably either Greek or, as some experts have suggested, Phoenician. Its chief ornamentation, at any rate, was a series of long panels, in which were cut the ancient Phoenican swastika. That was a symbol, I understand, of good luck. The topmost section was a replica of a Chinese pagoda. Needless to say, the entire structure was made of the finest Suffolk County white pine, chosen and seasoned by our own shipbuilders, and every inch of it was hand-carved." Dr. Tillinghast shook his head. "No," he said, "I hardly think that you or any person with a feeling for beauty would have called our steeple 'fantastic.' "

"Is there any prospect of restoring it?" I asked.

"We talk about it," Mr. Crawford said. " A year or two ago, we even had an architect out from New York to look into it. He said it could be done. There are plenty of good photographs of the old steeple around that an expert could go by. There hasn't been so much talk of it since we got his estimate, though. It was a little

over seventy-five thousand dollars." Mr. Crawford un-
locked the center door, pushed it open, and waved us
in. "That's just about five times the original cost of the
whole church."

We entered the lobby, big and square and gloomy.
Opening off it were three paneled oak doors leading to
the auditorium and the flanking pylons. The walls were
dark and hung with marble memorial plaques, one of
which read:

REV. SAMUEL KING,
A *Native of England,*
who departed this life Nov. 29th 1833;
after having ministered to this
congregation
one year and three months,
in the 42 year of his life.

THIS TABLET
as a token of respect
is devoted to the memory of a stranger and
a good man.
"The memory of the just is blessed."

Mounted on a low wooden frame in the middle of the
lobby was a mighty bell. Dr. Tillinghast caught up a
knotted end of rope attached to it as we passed. "Listen
to this tone," he said, and struck the bell a savage whack.
It gave an exhausted moan. "Sound as a dollar," he said.
"I venture to say not many bells could survive such a
fall."

"God spared what He deemed essential," Mr. Craw-ford said. "If you like, I'll take you up on the bell deck — what used to be the bell deck — before we leave. But right now . . ." He opened the auditorium door and took me by the arm. The three of us stepped into a silent immensity of whiteness. At the foot of a long center aisle, carpeted in faded green and lined with boxed pews, was a high rostrum. It was set in a *trompe-l'œil* circular arcade, flanked on either side by a door, and framed by a pair of round, fluted Corinthian columns and two square pilasters that rose, well over fifty feet, to a coffered ceiling. Two steeply inclined overhanging galleries, faced with an intricate frieze of carved volutes and rosettes, ran the length of the side walls. Behind each of them was a row of tall, tinted windows, ablaze with frosty lavender light. Except for the carpet, three tortuous black chairs on the rostrum, and a narrow trimming of rich, red mahogany along the sides and backs of the pews, the en-tire chamber was salt-white, and they made it look even whiter. For an instant, it was as dazzling as sun on snow.

Mr. Crawford dropped his hand from my arm. "It's beautiful, isn't it?" he said. "I don't mean to seem proud." I said, quite truthfully, that I'd never seen a more handsome room. "No," he said. "Of course, it's a few sizes too big for us now. I guess it always was. The sad thing is that it was built for the future. A hundred years ago, you know, there was a tremendous religious revival sweeping the country, and at the same time Sag

Harbor was getting more prosperous every year. We had the main floor pretty well filled for our centennial celebration. Maybe someday . . ." He sighed and smiled. "Those doors on either side of the platform go into the Sunday school. That's a good, big room, too."

"The Sunday-school annex is a later addition," Dr. Tillinghast said, without interest. Moving briskly down the aisle, he continued, "Let me call your attention to the fine Cuban-mahogany trimming on these pews — a very unusual touch. One of our whaling captains selected the wood himself in Cuba and brought it home in his own ship. The workmanship is that of shipwrights. You may have seen some photographs of old ships' railings that resembled it. And notice the little silver nameplates and numerals on the pew doors. That's another pretty touch. Up to about the Civil War, I understand, every pew was also furnished with a fine brass spittoon. Those old Sag Harbor whalers were a rough lot." He shook his head with a kind of admiration and pointed up at the wall. "I mentioned the Phoenician-swastika motif," he went on. "Well, there it is again, in that frieze just under the ceiling. Also, the columns supporting the galleries are exactly like those that formed the colonnade in the Sir Christopher Wren section of the steeple. You see how perfectly Lafever tied everything together?"

"There's another example of it, up there in the choir loft," Mr. Crawford said, turning back toward the lobby. He nodded in the direction of a third, and smaller, gallery, which linked the two side ones just above the door to the lobby. In a niche in the wall behind it stood what appeared to be a replica in miniature of the church's towering façade. I could even make out a row of tiny blubber spades around the parapets. "Our organ," he said. "You can see the pipes through those vents in the casing." He glanced at his watch. "If we're going up on the bell deck, we'd better get started. It's a good climb. How about you, Doctor?"

"You flatter me, Donald," Dr. Tillinghast said. "I'll try to content myself here below. I think, in fact, I'll sit down."

We left Dr. Tillinghast, looking wistfully after us, among the melancholy plaques in the vestibule. A circular staircase in the pylon to the right led us up to a bare anteroom on the gallery level. We went through a door into the choir loft, where there was another door, about the size of a transom, leading into the base of the tower. Mr. Crawford squirmed through this one. "I don't know who designed this," he said, "but he must have been thinking of a porthole." I followed him into a cobwebby cubicle behind the organ niche. It was not quite pitch-dark. "Watch yourself, now," he said. "These steps are steep." We went up two angular flights to a twilit landing, where Mr. Crawford directed my hand to the rail of an almost perpendicular stepladder. Then he disappeared overhead, breathing hard. I felt my

way slowly after him to another landing and another
ladder. We were well up in the tower now, and I could
hear the sound of the wind outside. Light appeared
above, and broadened into a tinted window, extending
a foot or two above the level of a third landing, where
we found ourselves in a forest of bare joists, beams, and
uprights. On one of the uprights was painstakingly
carved "J.M.F., Sept. 27, 1862." Mr. Crawford leaned
limply against a foot-square, hand-hewn pillar. It was
anchored, like a mast, in a thick, cast-iron shoe bolted to
a wooden girder. "This was one of the steeple supports,"
he said, giving it an indifferent pat. "The only one that
held. It snapped off higher up. The others sailed away
with the steeple. Listen to that wind up there. They tell
me the steeple used to shake like a tree on a day like
this. One more climb and we'll be in the middle of that
gale." He moved off along a catwalk of teetering planks.
It ended at the foot of a runged ladder, which rose some
twenty feet to a trapdoor in the ceiling. The ladder was
as unsteady as a rope as I followed him up. "Hold your
hat," he said, and heaved back the trap. We stepped out,
coattails flying and trousers flapping, onto a creaking tin
roof. It seemed like the top of the world.

We gazed down, over roofs and treetops and the spires
of three humbler churches at the deserted harbor. Beyond it lay the gray-green plain of the sea and the hazy
gray sand bluffs of faraway points and islands. "That's
Shelter Island, straight ahead," Mr. Crawford said,

hunching deeper into his coat. "Over there to the left of it is Noyack Bay. The smudge in the distance is the north fluke of Long Island — we're about on a line here with Greenport. That's another old whaling ruin. Off to the right, there, you can see the Rhode Island shore on a good, bright day."

I said it was quite a view. "It must have been magnificent from the top of the old steeple," I added.

"I suppose so," Mr. Crawford said. He turned and looked at me. "I suppose," he went on, "you noticed that our organ casing hasn't got a steeple. It was made that way. Prophetic, wasn't it?" There was an odd expression on his face. "I'll tell you what I think," he said. "Our steeple wasn't blown down by accident. These people here had got so they were worshiping the steeple more than they did God. So He took it away."

The Old Man's Chair

LAMBERT HITCHCOCK, a backwoods chairmaker who died, unencumbered by wealth or celebrity, in Unionville, Connecticut, in 1852, is now recognized by many antiquarians as one of the most artful of Early American craftsmen. Some do not hesitate to rank his work with that of the Shakers and the Pennsylvania Dutch. Hitchcock turned out a broad-minded assortment of chairs, including Boston rockers and cradle settees, but it is for a small, armless straightback of distinctive design that he is chiefly esteemed. Hundreds of these chairs, which he put together with the help of a few devoted artisans and several dozen women and children, have been pried out of old attics and upcountry kitchens in recent years. It is probable that he made thousands. Practically all were produced in what is now the Connecticut village of Riverton. Riverton is situated in a lonely glen in the Berkshires foothills, twenty-four miles northwest of Hartford, and straddles the west branch of the Farmington River. The village grew up around a factory that Hitchcock built on the riverbank in the early eighteen-twenties; it was once called Hitchcocks-ville, and its population, which has not perceptibly fluctuated for a century, is two hundred and one. The factory slipped from Hitch-cock's hands, which had been numbed by bankruptcy, shortly before his death. During the last half of the nine-teenth century, it was occupied by a firm of rule makers. Around 1910, a step-stool manufacturer took it over for a couple of years. After that, the building stood empty until the late twenties, when a maker of rubber nipples moved hurriedly in and out. Then it was abandoned to the wind and the weather. A tottering wing that over-hung the river was washed away in the floods of 1938. By that time, the floors had fallen in, weeds were growing in the cellar, and a creeper had unhinged the front door. It would probably be a hopeless ruin by now but for two West Hartford businessmen — John T. Kenney and Richard Coombs. Mr. Kenney is the proprietor of a shoe store, and Mr. Coombs is a building contractor. They acquired the old place in the autumn of 1946, and they have arrested its decline and reconverted it to the pro-duction of Hitchcock's little straightbacks.

One sleepy summer afternoon, I drove up to Con-necticut to see these men and their chairs. It was about three o'clock when I pitched down from the encir-cling hills, over a bridge, and into Riverton's elm-shad-owed main street, and the village was at rest. Even the factory had a look of repose. The factory is the first building on the west side of the river, and it is still a sub-stantial one. A broad structure, three shallow stories

high, it is made of brick, recently whitewashed, with a
low, peaked roof surmounted by a cupola and a huge,
immobilized weather vane. At one end a narrow, two-
story ell juts out in front. A door in the ell opens almost
on the street. Near it is a metal sign, erected by the State
of Connecticut, that reads: IN THIS FACTORY LAMBERT
HITCHCOCK MADE HIS FAMOUS HITCHCOCK CHAIRS, 1826–
1840. On the door, there is another, and more hospitable,
sign: VISITORS WELCOME — WALK IN. I pulled up under a
shaggy tree that must have given shade in Hitchcock's
day, and got out. A dissipated cat dozing on the stoop
was the only living creature in sight, and the only sound
was the soft harangue of the river.

The door was ajar. I stepped over the cat and into a
long, densely furnished room with a beamed ceiling and
a red plank floor. An enclosed staircase rose to the right
of the front door, and at the far end of the room there
was another door, leading to the main part of the building. The walls were calcimined and hung with framed
pages of early-nineteenth-century issues of the *Connecticut Courant*. In a corner by the stairs was a sagging
bookcase loaded with copies of old *Courants*, bound in
rusty leather. Across from it was a noble Boston rocker
and an urn full of cattails. A big, dilapidated wooden
foot-treadle lathe was propped up in another corner, and
there was a row of old carpenter's planes on a shelf just
above it. Under a window stood a long-legged, glass-
topped display case containing a collection of battered

ledgers, faded letters, and dog-eared books. The rest of
the room was crammed with Hitchcock chairs. There
were at least a dozen of them; all but two were obviously
brand-new, and all were a more or less identical blend of
Sheraton prettiness and rustic practicality. All were
painted a satiny black, enlivened here and there by a few
faint rose-colored ripples of graining, and their seats were
of woven natural rush. The front legs, the rung that ran
between them, and an arched cylindrical top piece that
joined the back posts were elegantly turned and tapered,
and these, and a broad, fretted, slightly concave horizontal center back slat, were decorated with stylized designs
— stars, flowers, leaves, fruit, or spread eagles — stenciled
in gold. The back legs were as plain as a hoe handle. Loll-
ing on one of the chairs was another, or possibly the
same, cat, and we had the room to ourselves.

I waited a moment, gazing at the chairs, and then
turned back toward the front door to see if there was a
bell or a knocker. Before I got there, the other door
banged open, and an elderly man with a stained mustache, and a pair of spectacles perched on his forehead,
stuck his head in. "Doggone it, Dick!" he shouted.
"Those . . ." He stopped. "Pardon me," he said, lowering his glasses and his voice. "You've got a walk on you
just like Dick's — Mr. Coombs." I told him I was looking for Mr. Coombs or Mr. Kenney myself. "They're
around," he said. "Those boys do everything but sleep
here, and I've known them to do that. I understand

they've got to keep introducing themselves to their wives. If I find Dick, I'll send him in. Jack's probably up in the office. They expecting you?" I said they were. "What did you say your name was?" he asked. I told him. "Uh-huh," he said. "Well, make yourself comfortable. Have a chair." He chuckled, pulled in his head, and slammed the door. The lathe groaned and settled a little. I took a chair.

Presently somebody walked across the floor overhead. There was a thump of heels on the stairs, and Mr. Kenney, a graying man of about forty, with tired eyes and an expression of haggard animation, ducked into the room. He is six feet six, and the top of his head almost brushed the ceiling beams. He had on a gray flannel shirt, a pair of dandelion-yellow suspenders, and baggy brown trousers, and he was tenderly massaging his left ear. "Vamoose!" he said, addressing the cat. The cat gave him a look and slid under the Boston rocker. "O.K.," Mr. Kenney said. Then he grinned at me, and came over and dropped heavily and confidently down on a chair. "Greetings," he said. "Sorry you had to wait. I saw you come in, but I was stuck on the phone — Macy's. They're our main New York outlet. Not that we've got much to let out yet. We will, though. It won't be long now." His eyes wandered around the crowded room. "I guess you've had time to look things over," he went on. "Those two down there at the end are old Lambert's. All the rest are

ours. Except the rocker, of course. I don't know how
much you know about furniture, but . . ." He hesitated, and nodded toward one of his chairs. "I mean —
well, what do you think of it? What's your impression?"

I said I thought it was a handsome chair. "It's certainly a remarkably faithful reproduction," I added.

Mr. Kenney gave a hollow laugh. "Thanks," he said,
"but I guess you don't understand. Hardly anybody does
at first. I'd better explain. The point is, our chair isn't a
reproduction. We don't make reproductions. That's the
whole idea. Our chair isn't *a* Hitchcock chair. The
market's swamped with that kind of trash. We've got a
couple down in the cellar. If that was the best we could
do, I'd be ashamed to look you in the face. We make *the*
Hitchcock chair. It's the old man's own chair. We've re-
created it. It's his chair from top to bottom, inside out,
and in between. The only difference between those two
over there and the pair we're sitting on is that these are
new. Otherwise, they're one and the same. Why, if old
Lambert himself strolled in here this afternoon, I doubt
if even he'd be able to tell them apart. Did you happen
to notice this?" He stood up and swung his chair around.
Stenciled in gold along the back of the seat frame was
an inscription: *L. Hitchcock. Hitchcocks-ville. Conn.
Warranted.* "The old man's trademark," he said. "We've
applied for permission to use it. Meanwhile, we're going
ahead. The way I look at it, it's just part of the chair.
The next thing I want to get is the real name of the

village restored. Then we'll have everything back just about the way it was in old Lambert's time. That's my dream."

Mr. Kenney let himself down astride the chair, lighted a cigarette, and folded his arms on the top piece. He shook his head. "To tell you the truth," he said, "this whole thing has been like a dream. I don't know how it happened. It was a miracle. I first laid eyes on this old building on the fourteenth day of July, 1946. That's one date I'll never forget. I was standing down there in the river fishing for trout, and I looked up and saw it. You never saw a more tumble-down place in your life. I got to wondering what it was. So I waded over this way to get a better look at it. I was just curious. And then I saw that marker that's out front. Brother, that gave me a chill. I felt weak. I knew a little about Hitchcock chairs, or thought I did. They amounted to something — I knew that. As a matter of fact, I had one. My wife and I got it for a wedding present. A beauty, too. Just like the one you're sitting on. But I'd never dreamed that Riverton was Hitchcocks-ville, or that the old Hitchcock factory was still standing. You know what I mean — I'd never even thought about it. All I thought about in those days was shoes — Palter Deliso, Delman, La Valle, and La so on. I'm surprised I can still remember the names. My brother's running the store for me now. Well, anyway, there was the factory, just waiting for somebody with vision to walk in and start it up again. I didn't know any more about making chairs than the man in the moon, if as much, but it didn't take me thirty minutes to realize that I'd walked right smack into the chance of a lifetime. It was like an inspiration. I made some inquiries and found out the building was owned by a woman here in the village. When I got back home, to West Hartford, I headed straight for Dick Coombs and told him about it. I've known Dick a long time, and I wanted him to come in with me. I needed him. Dick was a carpenter and cabinetmaker before he went into building, and he knows wood. He came right in. All he said was 'When do we start?' We started in August. That's how sure we were. I did talk to a couple of furniture dealers first, and I didn't hear a discouraging word. One of them wanted forty eagle-backs the week after next."

There was the sudden rumble of a truck on the bridge. Mr. Kenney froze. For an instant, the room shook with a quaking thunder. Then the sound diminished and slowly died away. "Thought that might be Jordan Marsh, up in Boston." Mr. Kenney said, relaxing. "I'm half expecting their van, and I don't know that we're ready. Distribution is what licked old Lambert, but that's one problem we don't have to worry about. Never did. It breaks your heart to read some of his records. They're in that case there. We've got a wonderful collection of Hitchcockiana. The old man could make up to fifty chairs a day, and more than once he rode horseback all the way to Chicago and St. Louis, taking orders, but he couldn't get them to the customer fast enough. He had to haul them by team over these hills twenty-four miles to Hartford. That was at least an all-day trip in his time. If he was lucky, he'd find a steamboat there to put them on. Then he had to wait for his dollar and a half — that was his price — to come back the same way. The chair itself was our problem, and production still is. I almost hate to tell you when we made our first chair. It wasn't until the fifteenth day of September, 1948. For a while, the best we could do was three a day. Right now, we're turning out around a dozen, but we'll double that soon. We've only got about fifteen people here, when they all show up. Two dozen a day, though, and we'd be on our way out of the red. Our chairs retail at forty dollars — thirty-nine ninety-five, to be exact — and the dealers get a big discount. We sell some by mail and hope to sell more that way. Then I'll begin to breathe easier. That first chair cost Dick and me close to forty-five thousand dollars." Mr. Kenney crushed out his cigarette. "But don't you worry, brother. We're right, and we know we're right. We've re-created the Hitchcock chair." He stood up. "Let's go find Dick," he said. "He ought to be out in the shop."

Mr. Kenney snapped his suspenders, and struck off down the room to the rear door, stepping nimbly over a hindering chair. I caught up with him at the door. Beyond it was a short passage. We emerged from that, under a precipice of piled lumber, into a vast thicket of angular lathes and drill presses, tool-strewn workbenches, and teetering tiers of partly assembled chairs. Sawdust and shavings littered the floor, and the air was heavy with the sultry smell of seasoned wood. Somewhere, deep in the room, a lathe was whining, but all the machines in sight stood idle and unattended, and the benches were deserted. Between a flight of stairs and a row of windows that overlooked the river I caught a glimpse of the elderly man with the stained mustache, shuffling along a labyrinthine path. His arms were loaded with what looked like kindling. "Everybody must be out for a smoke," Mr. Kenney remarked, craning his neck. "I wonder if Dick is. This is the woodworking shop. All the parts are fabricated and assembled here, except the seats. The seating department is on the next floor. The painting and decorating is all done up on the third, and that's where the finished chairs are stored. Smells good in here, doesn't it? I love the smell of good old Connecticut rock maple. That's all we use, from start to finish. Just like the old man did." He cupped his hands and called "Dick?" There was an instant answering growl. "Aha!" Mr. Kenney said. "This way."

We found Mr. Coombs, in a blue serge suit, contentedly tinkering with a mountainous hydraulic press at the far end of the room. A gray cat squatted on a box nearby, watching him. Mr. Coombs is nearly sixty, thickset, red-faced, tousle-haired, and heavy-jawed, and he has

a bristling pepper-and-salt mustache. His voice is harsh
and gravelly. In the First World War, he served under
the then Colonel George S. Patton, Jr., whom he reveres,
as a first sergeant, and he still looks like one. "Well, sir,"
he said, locking my hand in a granite grip, "I heard you
were here. One of the boys just told me. Has John been
taking good care of you?. . . Fine. John knows every
move old Lambert ever made." He released my hand
and added, "How do you like the chair?" Mr. Kenney
gently cleared his throat. I said I liked it very much.
"Fine," Mr. Coombs said. "Exactly. Yes. There are still
a couple of little questions I'd like to ask the old man, but
on the whole I'm thoroughly satisfied. It was a monstrous
job, though — the building as well as the chair. You
might say we re-created them both. Eh, John?"

"Dick deserves all the credit," Mr. Kenney said. "He
and Stafford Broughton. Staff is our head cabinetmaker.
Brother, he's a wizard. You'll meet him."

Mr. Coombs nodded. "Yes, sir," he said. "I'm thoroughly satisfied with the chair. The old man would approve of it. No doubt about that. Not the slightest. It's
the true Hitchcock. It looks like one, and it's made like
one, and it will hold up like one."

"We know it'll hold up," Mr. Kenney said, and
grinned. "Dick proved that one day. How about it,
Dick?"

"I did," Mr. Coombs replied. "Somebody told me
once that the sure test for a chair was to drop it out a

second-story window. If it's a good chair, it'll stay together. Well, sir, I sneaked over here late one Saturday and heaved one of ours out a window on the *third* floor. I thought I'd make good and sure while I was at it. It quivered when it hit, but it held. Didn't seem to faze it. Most chairs you see now start going wiggly-waggly after you've just sat on them a few months."

"There's another test that's a little easier," Mr. Kenney said. "I could show you if I had a chair handy. What you do is just lift it up by the top piece and let it fall on one of the legs. A good chair like ours will give a nice, springy bounce. The ordinary chair lands flat-footed."

"It's all you can do to pull one of the old man's chairs apart," Mr. Coombs said. "That's a fact. I know because I've done it. I knocked down two or three dozen or more originals our first year, trying to figure out what made them work. He was a marvel. John found one up in New Hampshire that had been used for a sawhorse ever since the Civil War. The seat was out, and the paint was mostly off, but there wasn't a crack in it. The way he put a chair together, the solid wood would give about as soon as the joint. You can say the same for ours. It's the same chair. There isn't a particle of difference. No, sir. He used water power to turn his lathes and we use electricity, but the chair's the same. There're twenty separate pieces of wood in the true Hitchcock — twenty-one, if it has two back slats — and we've matched them, piece for piece. I'm not going to name them, though, or tell you how we do it. If there's somebody out in Grand Rapids who wants to know, he can go to all the trouble John and Staff and I did."

"I doubt if they'd take the trouble even if they knew," Mr. Kenney said. "They haven't got old Lambert's factory anyway, or his trademark."

"I doubt it, too," Mr. Coombs said. "Nevertheless. But I will say this much. We fabricate every part exactly the way the old man did. We turn where he turned, we saw where he sawed, we steam and bend when he steamed and bent, we glue where he glued, and where he put a screw, we put one. We even dub off the points of our screws, just the way he did, so they'll hold better. That's something you don't often see any more, but common sense will tell you that the grip of a screw is all in the threads. And we use green wood here and seasoned wood there. That was another of his little tricks. When green wood shrinks around a seasoned dowel, you've got a joint only an axe can unlock. I don't mind telling you that, because it's a whole lot easier to say than do. Guesswork won't take you very far when it comes to allowing for shrinkage."

Mr. Coombs stared impassively at me for a moment. Then he uttered an agreeable grunt and slapped the flank of the big press. "This started out in life as a cider press," he said. "I found it in an old garage in Hartford. It's capable of five tons of pressure, and it's made to order for bending wood. We use it to put the curve in our back slats. I don't know how the old man did his bending. That's one of the questions I'd like to ask him. The other is how he made his bolster top pieces."

"I'd better explain," Mr. Kenney said, turning to me. "We make two styles of top pieces — the bolster and the crown. We'll have another before long, I hope. It's called the pillow. Right now, we're concentrating mostly on the bolster. All the chairs you saw up front were bolsters."

"Exactly," Mr. Coombs said. "There isn't much to the crown. It looks a lot like a back slat, and it isn't any harder to make. The bolster was our real problem. You must have noticed the fancy turnings on it, and if you looked close, you probably saw that it curves two ways. It arches up and it also curves back just a trifle. It's sawed roughly into shape — the old man never bent the bolster — and then it's turned. It's turned *after* it's shaped. Imagine trying to turn a curved piece of wood!"

"Oh, brother!" Mr. Kenney said, with respect.

I nodded, but I must have looked blank, because Mr. Coombs frowned. "Well, I'll give you an idea," he said. "Come along."

He cut around the press and headed down the room. Mr. Kenney and I picked our way after him to a secluded corner where a frail young man with a black mustache was hunched over a turning lathe. He had a small, delicate chisel in his hand. In front of him, at about waist height, a cylindrical length of wood, one end of which was fixed in a socket in a revolving horizontal arm of the lathe, was spinning with the speed of light. As we came up, he reached out and touched it with his chisel — and instantly, in a tiny blast of dust, a deep ring appeared in the wood. Then he brushed his chisel along four or five inches of the free end of the stick. I recognized the delicate taper of a Hitchcock front leg.

"Meet Staff Broughton," Mr. Coombs said to me. "Staff licked the bolster for us. We've just been talking about that little problem, Staff."

"Oh, yes," Mr. Broughton said, glancing absently up from his work. "We had our troubles."

"To put it mildly," Mr. Kenney said.

Mr. Coombs grunted, and directed my attention to the lathe. "See what I mean?" he said. "A straight piece of wood revolves evenly. You can handle it. But just picture a curved piece in there. The end would naturally be moving in a circle. Well, Staff figured out a way to make up for that off-center revolution. Don't ask me how. That's our Number One secret."

Mr. Broughton said nothing. Instead, he touched the spinning leg again with his chisel, producing another ring.

"Looks like fun, doesn't it?" Mr. Kenney remarked to me.

"It *is* fun," Mr. Broughton murmured.

"It's an art," Mr. Coombs said.

We watched Mr. Broughton finished turning the leg. Then he released it from the lathe, tossed it into a box at his feet, and started contentedly in on another. He seemed to have forgotten us. At a sign from Mr. Kenney, we moved discreetly off, along a trail that led to the stairs. Mr. Kenney took the steps two at a time. When Mr. Coombs and I reached the second floor, we found him standing at the head of a long aisle flanked by haphazard rows of seatless chairs. Most of them were unpainted, but some were colored blood red. A man in overalls was crouching at the end of one of the rows, slapping red paint on a chair. Near him, in a clearing by a window, several young women were at work around a low table. Each had a red chair in front of her, into which she was languidly weaving a seat of crackling rush. They all giggled and waved when they saw us, and the painter lifted a bloody hand. My companions beamed.

"A fine bunch of girls," Mr. Coombs told me. "Happy as larks."

"Wonderful," Mr. Kenney said warmly. "You couldn't ask for better. They're nearly all from right here in the village. Why, two or three of those girls had great-grandmothers who worked for the old man. They feel at home here." He cleared his throat. "To be honest with you, though, seating is our big bottleneck. Just look at all these chairs. They've been standing here for a couple of weeks, some of them. The girls do the best they can, but even the fastest ones can't handle more than about three a day, if that. I'm not complaining, of course. Rush-seating takes time. It has to be done by hand, and it has to be done right. That's the way they do it. We got a man from down Danbury way — Joe LaCava, an expert — to teach them. We didn't know any more about rush-seating than the man in the moon, did we, Dick? We still don't. The girls had a terrible time at first. Poor Joe just about went crazy. He was here every day for over two months, struggling with them. Every afternoon at five o'clock, he would come into the office and resign. 'It's no use,' he'd say. 'They won't learn.' I always managed to calm him down. We'd get out the bottle."

"It must be getting close to five now," Mr. Coombs said.

Mr. Kenney laughed. "Well, Joe stayed with them," he said. "I don't mind saying he ended up proud of our girls. They know rush now like Dick knows wood."

"What kind of rush do you use?" I asked.

"Cattails," Mr. Kenney said. "There's nothing better. Besides, that's what the old man always used. We cut it ourselves, in the swamps just north of here. The owners don't mind — they're glad to have somebody clean out the stuff — but, brother, it's a real job. Those swamps are deep and mucky and full of snakes and snapping turtles. And hot. Rush has to be cut just before it begins to turn brown, and that means the last week in July or the first week in August. The swamps are steaming then. All we cut is the female plant. The male is the one that carries the tail, and it's too woody to plait. The female is all leaves." Mr. Kenney flung a final smile down the aisle and turned to a flight of stairs leading to the floor above. "Watch yourself, now," he said, bounding on ahead. "There's a lot of wet paint up here."

There was a small black puddle of it, as bright as patent leather, when Mr. Coombs and I reached the top of the stairs. In it lay an overturned can. Mr. Kenney was standing a short distance away, near a clump of glossy-black chairs, scraping the sole of his shoe on the floor and smiling ruefully. "No harm done, I guess," he said. "Quit grinning, Dick. It was practically empty. Well, let's get going." We skirted the cluster of chairs and came abruptly upon a young woman in dungarees reclining on the floor, painting a red chair black. Beyond her were more chairs, and beyond them, far down the room, were three men at a row of worktables. She twisted her head around, blew a frond of hair out of her eyes, and gave us a pleasant stare as we passed. "A fine girl," Mr. Coombs observed. "Yes, sir. She's a real professional." He scowled about him with interest and satisfaction. "I haven't been up here in a coon's age," he said.

"Dick sticks pretty close to the shop," Mr. Kenney told me. He slackened his pace. "I guess you noticed that girl was using a brush. So was the bird downstairs who puts on the undercoat. We don't believe in spraying paint. You have to use a brush to get the true Hitchcock effect. Incidentally, there's a good reason why the undercoat is red. It gives a nice glow to the chair, especially when the black gets worn down a little. The old man wanted his chair to look like rosewood. Not real rose-wood, of course — he wasn't trying to fool anybody. I mean he wanted it to look the way rosewood ought to look. Talk about art! That's the reason for the red grain-ing, too."

"Old Lambert had a reason for everything he did," Mr. Coombs said. "You don't have to pull very many of his chairs apart to find that out."

We left the chairs and went over toward the men at the tables. Two of them had their backs to us. The other nodded to us across the seat of a chair he was working on. He was an aging young man with a round face and pale hair, and he wore a flowing Windsor tie. A paint-brush was stuck in the corner of his mouth, like a frayed cigar. Mr. Kenney raised a long arm in greeting. "George Slater," he said to me. "Our head decorator. The old man had women decorators, but we just couldn't find any good enough."

"I don't worry about that," Mr. Coombs said.

"Maybe women were different in those days," Mr. Kenney said. "It doesn't bother me, either. Anyway, we know that the old man worked out all the designs and cut all the stencils himself. George re-created the designs for us, and he does all the stenciling. The other boys do the rest of the decorating. They put the gilt banding on the turnings and brush in the graining. Stenciling is the big thing. When George gets finished with a chair, it's all done except for varnishing. I want you to meet him."

He led me over to Mr. Slater. "George cut the stencil for the trademark, too," he said as he introduced us. "He's a real artist."

Mr. Coombs confirmed this with an emphatic grunt, but Mr. Slater cocked his head deprecatingly. "I used to be," he said. "Besides, there wasn't much to the trademark. Even if the lettering is a little special, it takes only one stencil, and only one tone of gold. The back-slat designs take about six stencils apiece, most of them, and as many different tones."

"I didn't know there *were* six different tones of gold," I said.

"No?" Mr. Slater said. "There're a dozen or more. All you need is enough gold powder, banana oil, and thinner, and you can make anything from red to white gold. The design that tried my patience was the eagle. It takes only five stencils, but I was a solid day breaking it down. It's an extremely clever design. But then they all are."

"Exactly," Mr. Coombs said. "One hundred per cent." He tapped his mustache and looked thoughtful. Then he said, "But George has his work to do, John. So maybe . . ."

Mr. Kenney laughed heartily. "I'm ready," he said.

We left Mr. Slater and headed for the office, on the second floor of the ell. A door at the end of the seating room led us into a kitchen, where Mr. Kenney got a pitcher of water and three tumblers. The office was just beyond — a small, dim, untidy room with a view of the dooryard and the shadowy depths of an elm. A golden-oak desk and a sway-backed swivel chair stood in one corner, a gaunt hatrack in another, and between the front windows, a table on which was a row of metal filing cabinets. Scattered about were several new Hitchcock chairs. The floorboards were bare and scuffed, there was a rambling water stain on the ceiling, and on the walls were a collection of old chair parts dangling from a string, two or three idyllic Currier & Ives prints of rural life, and the framed exhortation, "Think." Mr. Coombs shot a fierce glance at the stain. Then he shoved three chairs up to the table, waved me into one, sank down on the second, and crossed his legs on the third. Mr. Kenney was busying himself at the desk. We watched him pull open a deep drawer and take out a succession of empty whiskey bottles. Finally, he found one about two-thirds full.

When he had fixed us each a drink, he lowered himself cautiously into the swivel chair, lay back, and lighted a cigarette. Presently he sighed. We sipped our drinks in a companionable silence for a time.

"Peaceful," said Mr. Coombs, at last.

"Oh, brother!" Mr. Kenney murmured. He roused himself a trifle. "One of these days," he said, "you'll see me living here. I've already got my land. It's on the slope

up across from the Congregational Church. The hell
with West Hartford and the shoe business and all the
rest of it. If a fellow couldn't live here and like it, there's
something plenty wrong with him. This is traditional —
the Hitchcock chair, Hitchcocks-ville, the old Hitchcock
factory. I don't know. There's a satisfaction in it. For a
fellow like me, anyway." He took a thoughtful swallow of
his drink. "Dick knows all this," he went on, "but I
wasn't born to any gold spoon. My father was a dentist,
up in Northampton, Mass., and he died when I was sixteen. I didn't get to college. I went to work in my uncle's
shoe store up there, instead. I was supporting my mother
and my sister and two brothers when I was seventeen.
By the time I was nineteen, I had a store of my own in
Poughkeepsie and another in Wellesley. They both
folded up in 1938. I borrowed some money and started
one in West Hartford. I was married then, with a baby,
and I still had my mother and my sister and my brothers.
The first year in West Hartford, I did twenty-eight thousand dollars' worth of business. When I turned the store
over to my brother, a while back, it was doing close to
half a million a year. But it was just a business. I mean
it was what anybody could have if he wanted to work
for it the way I did. What I wanted was something real.
You might call it an inheritance. All I ever got or in-
herited was hard work. I used to see those friends of
mine who were born to the purple — I was working day
and night, including Sundays. Well, then I stumbled on

this. It's given me what I always wanted. There's something real here, and traditional." He shrugged. "I don't know. You can be proud of it."

Mr. Coombs made a sympathetic sound and scowled into his glass. "I guess I just wanted to make that pretty little chair," he said.

The Delectable Mountains

ONE late-September afternoon, I drove out to a flat, sandy, frequently fog-drenched farm on the southeastern shore of Long Island, near the village of Bridgehampton, and gave myself the pleasure of an hour or two in the company of a contented potato grower named George C. Strong. Mr. Strong's farm consists of a hundred and fifty explosively fecund acres, but the peace of mind that he commonly enjoys does not result entirely from the reasonable certainty of profit they give him. The fact is that, unlike many of his confreres, he has a high personal regard for the potato. Twice a day, at lunch and dinnertime, his devotion to it borders on the reverential. Mr. Strong is discriminating in his approach to his favorite delicacy. There are numerous varieties of the white, or Irish, potato. The most generally admired, in this country, are the Katahdin, Pontiac, Chippewa, Rural, Earlaine No. 2, Mohawk, Houma, Irish Cobbler, Erie, Sebago, Warba, Sequoia, Russet Burbank, and Green Mountain. Mr. Strong raises nothing but Green Mountains. He believes that this variety is not only supreme among potatoes but the tastiest, the least cloying, and, with the possible exception of meat, the most nourishing of foods.

Mr. Strong's farm is less than two miles from the ocean. The day of my visit was cloud-hung and windy, and when I pulled up in front of his house I could hear a distant mumble of surf and there was a seaweedy smell in the air. The house is white, green-shuttered, and finickingly Dutch Colonial, with a high stoop, flanked by a pair of built-in benches, and a tidy lawn and privet hedge between it and the road. Off to one side is a substantial two-car garage, the only outbuilding in sight. The place has such a snug and oddly suburban look that the desolate plain of raw, muddy fields surrounding it could be taken for vacant building lots. I went up to the stoop and rang the bell, and a Negro maid opened the door. I said that Mr. Strong was expecting me. "Well, he's in the living room," she said. "Right through there."

I found Mr. Strong sitting on a sofa, smoking an after-luncheon cigar. He is a handsome, muscular, well-fed man of forty-five, with hair that is smooth, prematurely white, and slowly vanishing. He was wearing heavy brogans, tan duck trousers, and a tan cotton shirt. As I came in, he stood up and said amiably, "Hello, there. Glad to see you." Then he dropped abruptly back on the sofa. "Sit down," he said. "Make yourself comfortable. If it's all the same to you, I'd just as soon sit here and finish this cigar before we go out and take a look around." I let myself down into a deep armchair opposite him. It was an easygoing room, with a large brick fireplace and a somber oil painting, in a gilt frame, above the mantel. Bookshelves, crammed with books, papers, and pamphlets, lined part of one wall. Near them was a battered play pen, and in it a battered plush rabbit. In a corner stood a handsome spinet, with a copy of *Popular Mechanics* lying open on its rack. I lighted a cigarette and dropped the match in a clamshell ash tray at my elbow.

Mr. Strong studied me for a moment. Then he crossed his legs and said, "Now, I don't know how much you know about potatoes, but I wouldn't be surprised if you'd heard that Sir Walter Raleigh found the potato in Virginia and introduced it into England and the rest of Europe." I said that I had. Mr. Strong smiled, more in resignation than in triumph. "Well, there isn't a speck of truth in that," he said. "Raleigh may have introduced tobacco over there, but not potatoes. The first potatoes ever grown in America were planted by some Scotch-Irish settlers up at Londonderry, New Hampshire, in 1719. That's a fact. The potato isn't a native of this country at all. It's a native of Peru and Chile. The Spaniards found it down there around the middle of the sixteenth century, and they were the ones who gave it to the world. If you ask me, that's the greatest contribution to civilization that Spain ever made. The Indians who lived along the western

coast of South America had been growing potatoes on
the slopes of the Andes for centuries before the Spaniards got there. Potatoes were what they lived on. Nobody seems to know where those Indians got hold of
them. Not that it matters, though. The big pity is that
the world had to wait for it so long. Why, potatoes are
one of the few foods of any consequence that's turned
up since Biblical times. Not only that, but there isn't
any other important food, let alone one as cheap and
good and as easy to grow, that people were slower to
take to. When they finally did get the potato, almost
nobody would eat it. Not even the Spaniards."

Mr. Strong gave a cheerful snort and went on to say
that the potato was a wallflower for nearly two hundred
years after it had been transplanted to Europe. The ex-
otic origin of the plant alone was enough to make most
people leery of it. Many Protestant theologians, being
unable to uncover any reference to it in the Bible, de-
clared that it was unfit for Christian consumption.
About the only sixteenth-century potato-raisers, I gathered, were keepers of botanical gardens, who regarded
it as an interesting freak of nature, and a few princely
landowners of jaded, adventurous tastes. "The general
run of people thought potatoes looked ugly and tasted
worse," Mr. Strong said. "Maybe in those days they were
ugly, but I doubt it. We haven't improved the breed
that much. Also, the idea got around that they were
probably poisonous. I won't deny that there was some

reason for that, at first. The potato *is* a member of the deadly-nightshade family of plants, and certain other members of that group have narcotic properties, so I suppose people just jumped to conclusions. Anyway, that suspicion was cleared up soon enough. After all, potatoes were being eaten to some extent in Europe even then, and nobody was falling down dead at the supper table. My guess is that the potato would have been going strong by the middle of the seventeenth century if it hadn't been for the doctors. They were the ones who did the real harm. First of all, they said it was a dangerous aphrodisiac. Then they gradually worked around to blaming it for lots of bad diseases. They said it was the cause of leprosy and the cause of syphilis and the cause of I don't know what all. Why, up to about the time of Napoleon, doctors were still insisting that eating a potato would give you indigestion."

I asked Mr. Strong what had finally made people change their minds. "Misery," he replied. "Plain misery. So far as I know, the potato is the only blessing in history that mankind had to be driven to. The Irish were the first to warm up to it. They were the first nation to raise potatoes as a field crop — in a serious way, at any rate. That was somewhere in the sixteen-fifties. Potatoes did a lot for the Irish. The peasants didn't have the land it takes to raise enough of other crops, but they found that they could grow more potatoes than they could eat on what land they had. This increased the birth rate so

much that pretty soon Ireland had a population almost
half the size of England's, and the Irish developed a
sense of importance and that proud way of theirs toward
the Crown that they've kept to this day. Then, in 1845,
the potato blight came along. Within a few years two
million Irishmen had either died or left the country, and
the whole idea of Ireland's becoming a big, strong nation blew up. But for a while there, potatoes might easily
have changed the course of world history. It's no wonder
they're called Irish potatoes. By the way, everything
about that name is wrong. They aren't any more Irish
than cabbage is. And, from one way of looking at it, they
aren't even potatoes. What we call the sweet potato is
the original potato — *Ipomoea batatas.*" He spelled it
out for me. "That's a mixup that goes right back to the
beginning, to the middle of the sixteenth century. There
are two or three versions of exactly what happened, but
according to most authorities the two plants were discovered at about the same time. The sweet potato was
found in the West Indies by another bunch of Spaniards. For a while everybody thought that the sweet potato and the South American potato were related.
They're not, even distantly. The name — it's an English
corruption of *batatas*, the West Indian word for sweet
potatoes — is the only thing the two have in common.
The white potato is *Solanum tuberosum*, which, as you
can see, has nothing to do with its English name at all.
But about Ireland. The fact that the Irish were the first

to appreciate white potatoes doesn't mean that they were any smarter or braver than other people. They were just hungrier. Most people in most other countries, including America, didn't get that hungry until well along in the next century. The seventeen-hundreds were full of commotion, you know — wars, rebellions, famines, and especially the Industrial Revolution, which disrupted everything. There's no getting around it; hard times are what it took to make potatoes popular. People just couldn't afford not to eat them. After all, you put away a plateful of potatoes and you know you've had a meal.

"I told you that potatoes are easy to grow. Well, for a cultivated plant, they're unique. Nothing can touch them — wheat, corn, rice, or anything. They grow almost like weeds. The only thing I ever heard of that can match a potato plant in producing is a pair of rabbits. I'll give you an example. Wheat is the only crop that compares with potatoes in food value, and sixteen or eighteen bushels to the acre is a fair yield for wheat. Now, I've seen an acre of land produce *six hundred* bushels of potatoes. Three hundred and fifty or four hundred is not uncommon. Why, a man can raise enough potatoes in his own back yard to feed his family for close to a year. And he doesn't have to pay some miller to make them fit to eat, either. 'The poor man's bread' is what potatoes used to be called in the old days, and you can see why."

Mr. Strong pitched his cigar into the fireplace, stretched, sighed, and stood up. "We've just finished digging the last of our potatoes," he said, "so I've got nothing to do except sit here and talk and wait for supper, but maybe I'd better show you around a bit before we get too comfortable to move. The storage barns are down the road a ways. My place is kind of spread out, but that's the way I like it. I don't see any sense in living in the middle of a barnyard." We went out to the front hall, where he stopped to slip on a suède windbreaker and stick a jaunty ski cap on his head. While we were standing there, I heard voices upstairs. One of them was shrill and crotchety. Mr. Strong fondly cocked an ear. "That's our youngster," he told me. "My wife must be getting him up from his nap, and he likes to sleep. Jimmy's just two years old, but he'd be big for four. We've got four children — three boys and a girl — and they're all hefty. I don't mean fat. Just big, healthy potato eaters. This family doesn't *live* on potatoes, but it certainly eats its share."

"How much is that?" I asked.

"Oh, around thirty pounds a week, I'd say," he replied. "That's probably as much as the run of families this size will eat in a month. I'm not counting the colored girl. She isn't overly fond of potatoes. I guess you noticed that she's a little on the scrawny side." He laughed, and opened the door.

*   *   *

We cut across the lawn toward the road. Mr. Strong took a deep breath and hunched his shoulders against the wind. "Listen to that surf!" he exclaimed. "This kind of weather gives a man an appetite." He looked thoughtful for a moment. Then, as we turned in to the road, he said, "You know, a person *can* live on just potatoes. Or pretty near. I'm not advocating it, of course, but it's possible. It wouldn't be such a terrible hardship, either. I don't know any food it would take you longer to get tired of, the flavor is so light and gentle. But that isn't the main thing. Potatoes, to my way of thinking, come close to being a perfect food. The Irish proved that. Over there, the poor used to live for months at a time on only potatoes and a little milk. A potato is about four-fifths water, but there's plenty of goodness in that remaining one-fifth. Something like eighty-five per cent of the fifth is starch, and around five per cent is sugar. The rest is made up of potassium, phosphorus, calcium, iron, sodium, sulphur, and chlorine, among other things. It's got a lot of Vitamins C, B_1, and B_2 in it, too, and a little protein, but not enough, I'm sorry to say. The potatoes we grow out here by the ocean even have some iodine. Six or seven pounds of potatoes and a big glass of milk every day will give you all the food you need. The milk is to make up for the protein shortage and to provide Vitamins A and D. Those vitamins and fat are about the only things a potato hasn't got any of." Mr. Strong raised his voice a trifle. "I'll bet

you've heard all your life that potatoes are fattening,"
he said. "The health boobs are always spreading that
notion. People have been eating less and less potatoes in
the United States for the past twenty years, and I lay
it entirely to that. Even the vegetarians are getting scared
of potatoes. Sure, starch is fattening, but not if you don't
eat more than you need. The truth is, as any halfwit
should know, that almost anything will make you fat if
you stuff yourself with it. The really fattening thing
about potatoes is the butter or gravy that most people
put on them."

"Don't you like them with butter or gravy?" I asked.

Mr. Strong gave me an indulgent glance. "I like them
every way there is," he said. "I pity anybody who doesn't.
I like them baked, boiled, and mashed. I like them
creamed, browned, hash-browned, riced, French-fried,
and home-fried. I like them scalloped and I like them
au gratin, and if there are other ways, I like those, too.
I like potato cakes for breakfast in the wintertime and
I like potato salad in hot weather. The best bread I ever
ate was my mother's, and she always mixed some mashed
potatoes in with the flour. That bread was really fit to
eat. It was like angel cake. Some of the smoothest liquor
I ever drank was made from potatoes. If I had to choose,
though, I guess I'd take my potatoes either creamed or
just plain peeled, boiled, and sprinkled with salt." A
ravenous grin appeared on Mr. Strong's face, and he
shook his head. "I can't truthfully say that I've ever

really had my fill of boiled potatoes," he said, "and I could certainly stand a good helping of them right now." I began to feel a little hungry myself.

The road — humped, cratered, and surfaced with peeling asphalt — ran as straight as a furrow between dark, identical fields. It was an oppressive countryside. There was nothing to hold the eye — just the road, the fields, and the lowering sky. Mr. Strong had drifted into a retrospective, or perhaps anticipatory, silence, but presently he cleared his throat and said, "One nice thing about the kind of potatoes I raise is they're versatile in the kitchen, if you get what I mean. Green Mountains were developed in this country at least fifty years ago, and they're still the best all-round eating potato going. They bake up mealy and they boil solid. If you think just any potato will do that, you're badly mistaken. Those big Idahos you hear about all over the place — Russet Burbank is the real name — are good bakers, but they go all to pieces when they're boiled. It's the other way around with an ordinary good boiler. Bake it and you'll end up with a lump of soap. But Mountains are something else. They hit a pretty happy medium. They'll do anything a potato is supposed to do, and do it better than most. They've got what I call interior quality, and they've got a flavor all their own, too. It's delicious." He smiled faintly. "That isn't just my opinion. I'm not the only man who raises Mountains, you know. Not by a long shot. Close to half the growers here in Suffolk County raise Mountains, and this is the third-biggest potato-producing county in the United States. We produced more than nineteen million bushels last year — the only counties that can top us are Aroostook, up in Maine, and Kern, in California — and nine of those nineteen were Mountains.

"I won't pretend I was always smart enough to go in for Mountains," Mr. Strong continued comfortably and with the air of confessing some youthful peccadillo. "When I started out, back in 1927, I grew Chippewas. My father always grew them. He's a building contractor, or he was, but he used to raise a fair amount of potatoes on the side. Potato growing has been a habit with the Strongs and the Hands — that's my mother's family — for a long time. My people helped found Southampton in 1640 and they've been working with the potato ever since it hit this country. Dad has a place back up the road. This is called Strong's Lane, by the way. Dad went in for Chippewas because so many people have always been crazy about them. That's just because Chippewas look nice. No doubt about it, Chippewas are the smoothest, lightest-colored, shallowest-eyed, and best-looking potatoes on the market. But they're also the soggiest and the worst-tasting. There's no doubt about that, either, although Katahdins are a close second. Well, when I started growing Chippewas, I was just out of agricultural school up at Cornell, except that I'd wasted a couple of years in the real-estate business at Southampton and down in Florida, and I didn't know any better than to go in for Chippewas. Besides, Dad gave me a good part of the sixty-eight acres I began with, so it was natural to raise what he raised. I switched over to Mountains in the early thirties. I got disgusted with selling a potato that I didn't care much about eating. But that's not the only reason why I like to raise Mountains. It may be my imagination, but it seems to me that they do better in the kind of soil we have out here on the south fork of the Island than any other variety I know."

The soil on Mr. Strong's farm is, it seems, as remarkable as the Green Mountain potato and considerably less abundant. For potato raising, it is almost without equal. Soil of this sort occurs, in the United States, only in an area of about fifty square miles, extending from Southampton on the west to Amagansett on the east and from the ocean on the south to the Peconic Bays and Gardiners Bay on the north. The soil is known to Department of Agriculture agronomists as Bridgehampton Loam, since Bridgehampton is in approximately the center of the region. Bridgehampton Loam consists of silt, clay, and sand, and it is porous and moderately acid. Many other soils possess some or all of these constituents and characteristics, but not in precisely the same proportions. Any potato land in the Bridgehampton Loam area commands a price of at least a thousand dollars an acre.

"The federal crop program has potato prices pretty much fixed right now," Mr. Strong said. "But in the old days those of us in this neighborhood generally got as much as ten cents more for our potatoes than anybody else on the Island. That isn't a premium to sneeze at, and it gives you some idea how good this soil is. I've sold my potatoes for as high as two dollars a bushel. I've sold them for as little as thirty cents, too, during the depression, but even that was better than most growers got. The lowest yield I've ever had is two hundred and fifty bushels to the acre. The last two years I've averaged better than five hundred, and some of my fields did five seventy."

Mr. Strong went on to say, rather hurriedly, that he was by no means a rich man. His expenses, he assured me, are high. They average about two hundred and fifty dollars an acre annually. This includes taxes, labor (he employs two men the year around, six at planting time, and twelve during the harvest season), maintenance of equipment, insurance, and buying seed potatoes, fertilizer, insecticides, and disease-inhibiting sprays. "It costs real money to grow *good* potatoes," Mr. Strong said. "Spray is a big item. We get a lot of moisture out here, which is one reason why we produce such bumper crops, but fungus blight and insects thrive in this climate, too. During the growing season — from the middle of April to about Labor Day, that is — we have to spray the vines every five or six days. We control blight with a mixture of copper sulphate and hydrated lime. For insects, of course, we use DDT. We mix it in with the blight spray and shoot them on at the same time. I hear some scientists think that DDT may actually stimulate the growth of the plant, like fertilizer. It certainly seems to, but my hunch is that it simply kills off a lot of insects that we never used to even suspect were there. I lay the big yields we've been getting since the war chiefly to DDT, good seed, and tractors. Tractors speed everything up, and speed is what we need. It's devil take the hindmost when you're fighting bugs, blight, and weeds. That building you see way over yonder is my equipment barn." Mr. Strong pointed to a bleak gray corrugated-iron structure standing alone in the middle of a seemingly limitless field. It looked like a crossroads garage. "That barn started out as an airplane hangar," he said. "I used to fool around with a little Taylorcraft some years back. That was my hobby. Before that, I played the Hawaiian guitar — or at it. Now I'm going in for archery. Anyway, I got rid of my plane about the time I got rid of my horses. I was the first grower on the south fork to farm without horses. My place has been practically a hundred-percent mechanized since 1932 or '33. I've even got a machine to cut up seed potatoes for planting. The only living creatures on the place right now, except people, are a couple of cows that one of my men keeps to feed the culls to, and my wife's Manx cat. When I want an egg, I buy it. Except for a winter cover crop of rye, which

I plow under just before spring planting, all I raise or ever mean to raise is potatoes. They're enough to hold my interest."

I asked Mr. Strong why he buys seed potatoes. "Couldn't you use your own?" I said.

"I could," he replied, "but I'd be a fool to. I'll tell you why. I wouldn't get nearly the yield I do this way. Seed potatoes are a business in themselves. Most of the seed used here in the East is grown in upstate New York, in northern Maine, or on Prince Edward Island, up in Canada. The growing season is so short in those places that the potatoes never fully mature. The frost kills off the vine before they get a chance to. But here's the thing — it also kills off any disease that may have got started. The potatoes may not be ripe enough to eat, but they're capable of reproducing themselves and they're about as healthy as a potato can be. Then, before they're sold, they're inspected by plant pathologists to make sure they're still healthy. Well, when you plant certified disease-free seed, your chances of getting a good crop are considerable. A sound seed potato will produce up to twenty times its weight in eating potatoes." Mr. Strong lighted a cigarette, striking the match expertly on the seat of his trousers. "Of course," he said, "a potato isn't really a seed, or even, as a lot of people think, a root, which a sweet potato is. It's just an enlarged section of stem. You know how a willow slip will take root and sprout? A potato works the same way. The potato's real seeds develop from the blossoms up on the vine. They look like radish seeds. But nobody bothers with them except plant breeders who are out to work up new varieties, because they never reproduce true to type. If I planted the seeds from my vines, I'd be apt to get a crop of something nobody ever heard of."

We were almost upon the storage barns before I saw them — two long, squat, low-roofed sheds, facing the road and built into a gentle slope that rose from one side of it. Their sides were banked with earth right up to their eaves, which were overgrown with weedy grass. Only their doors and roofs were visible. Down the road beyond the barns was a brown, shingled bungalow, which Mr. Strong said was the home of one of his helpers. Three little Negro children were solemnly wrestling in the yard outside it, and Mr. Strong waved to them, but they were too busy to respond. He shrugged philosophically, went up to the door of the nearer barn, and swung it open. I followed him into a damp, cool, earthy-smelling darkness.

"It's no cinch to store potatoes," Mr. Strong told me, halting just inside the door, "but under proper conditions they'll keep about nine months. At least, Mountains will. You've got to realize that a potato is a living and breathing organism. There are four things that it can't stand after it's been dug — heat, freezing cold, sunlight, and dryness. Leave a potato on the ground for only an hour on a cloudy day when the temperature is around eighty-five, and it will blister. On even a mild day, if there's a bright sun, it will sunburn. That is, it will build up chlorophyll and turn green and bitter-tasting. We haul our potatoes into the barn as fast as possible during picking. If they freeze, they'll rot when they thaw, and low humidity shrivels them up. We keep it about forty degrees in here. Insulation does the trick in warm weather, and in winter we use a furnace. We've got a machine to keep the humidity at around ninety per cent."

Mr. Strong moved over to the wall and snapped on a light. I almost jumped. Instead of expanding in the light, the room seemed suddenly to contract. A dozen feet or so from the door rose a mighty, slatted crib, filled almost to the ridgepole with potatoes. Several small piles of potatoes in bushel bags flanked the entrance like boulders. Mr. Strong bent down and rummaged around in one of the bags. "I've got a total storage capacity of about forty-seven thousand bushels," he told me over his shoulders. "This barn holds close to thirty-five thousand alone, but it isn't quite full now, and neither is the other. We begin trucking potatoes to a dealer in Bridgehampton soon after we start digging, and we keep selling right through the winter, depending on the way prices are going. Prices generally go up a little toward spring, so it pays to hang on to some." He straightened up, holding an open pocketknife in his right hand and in his left a couple of potatoes, one of which he gave to me. "Nice, isn't it?" he said. "You'll have to take a bagful with you when you go. That pale-brown skin, that oblong shape, and those moderately deep eyes are the main characteristics of a Mountain. The main *visible* characteristics, I mean." I looked at my potato. It looked disappointingly like any other potato to me. But if my expression indicated my thoughts, Mr. Strong didn't notice. He had turned his attention to his potato and had cut off a generous slice. After peeling it, he popped it into his mouth. "Delicious," he murmured, serenely crunching. "Good and starchy. Would you care for a piece?"

Buckle and Tongue

I took an early train up to New Milford, Connecticut, one day in May and spent several placid hours with Percy Peck Beardsley, the leading raiser of purebred Devon oxen in the Northeast and quite possibly in the whole country. His farm, which is in the hills of Litchfield County, some twelve miles from the station, consists of two hundred high, sharply tilted acres of fine meadowland. Most of it was acquired by his great-grandfather in 1794. It is the only farm in the neighborhood that is owned and worked by a direct descendant of an original settler, and it looks as though its original settler might conceivably still be living on it.

Mr. Beardsley, a fifty-four-year-old bachelor who seldom budges from his farm any more, appeared to be enjoying the tepid bustle of New Milford when he met me at the depot. His face is long and square-jawed, his mouth wide and thin-lipped, and his hair thick, gray, and unruly. He is tall, solid, unexcitable, and more or less detached from the twentieth century. He had spruced up for the trip to town in a blue serge suit, a rather gaudily striped shirt, a necktie that seemed to be choking him, and a fawn-colored and obviously brand-new hat. I learned later that he owns a collection of hats that a boulevardier might well covet. A kindly cousin who works for one of the Danbury hat manufacturers keeps peppering him with the latest models. Mr. Beardsley accepts these gifts with more grace than gratitude and patiently stores them away in their stylish boxes behind a sofa in his parlor. Ordinarily, he wears a lumpy old tweed cap.

Mr. Beardsley welcomed me with a somnolent smile and a prolonged, numbing handshake. "Let's watch her pull out," he said, nodding toward the train. We watched her go. Then he loosened his necktie, sighed peacefully, and led me over to his car, a big, hard-breathing Buick sedan. "Well, sir," he said as it lumbered through town and headed into the hills, "I guess you know that the ox business isn't what it used to be. Be a wonder if it was, with all the science we've got around now. When Dad was my age — he died three years ago, at seventy-five — we generally had over seventy head of cattle on the place, and at the Danbury Fair in 1917 we *showed* fifty-two head. Right now, I've only got fifty. I keep a breeding stock of thirty head — two bulls and the rest cows and heifers. I sell around sixteen or so head — oxen and heifers — a year. That's not much more than half the number we used to sell in the old days. Lately, I've been getting so few orders for oxen that I've even had to sell a few head of steers for beef — something we never used to do. Our practice has always been to sell our heifers for breeding and the steers for working. A good breeding heifer is worth around two hundred and fifty dollars nowadays, and a matched yoke of oxen will bring up to about six hundred. Thirty years ago, we got right around double that. That's progress, I guess, so it can't be helped." He gave me a cheerful look and pushed his elegant hat back off his forehead. "Anyway," he added, "I'm still making buckle and tongue meet, as Dad used to say."

I gathered that Mr. Beardsley is relieved rather than exhilarated at having done as well as he has. This is not an unnatural reaction. His father, the late Nathan Beardsley; his grandfather, Thompson Beardsley; and his great-grandfather, Captain Nathan Beardsley, were also eminent breeders of Devons. For nearly a hundred and fifty years, Beardsley oxen — or working cattle, as farmers usually call them — have been monotonously consistent winners of first, second, and third prizes at county and state fairs, mostly in Connecticut and New York. Mr. Beardsley's great-grandfather, who served in the Revolutionary Army, was one of the pioneers in establishing the Devon strain in the United States. The accomplishments of his forebears gratify Mr. Beardsley intensely, but they also tend to make him self-conscious.

"Oh, there's still a market for oxen," he said firmly as he sawed the car around a wicked bend in the road and across a clattering bridge, and it seemed to me that he was trying to reassure himself as much as he was me. "A bigger market than you probably think," he went on as we began a painful climb up the side of a steep, wooded hill. "Now, just last week I sold a nice pair to a fellow." Whatever doubts Mr. Beardsley may have been entertaining appeared suddenly to vanish. A grin spread over his face, and he said, "Sold 'em to a fellow that makes tractors, too." I said that this must have given him a good deal of satisfaction. "Well, I won't say it didn't," he replied. "The fact is, the man was kind of shamefaced about it. 'I suppose you think I'm crazy,' he said, 'but I've got a lot of wood on my farm down in Virginia that's got to be hauled, and a tractor can't do the job.' " Pleased as Mr. Beardsley was by this admission, he was not particularly surprised by it. He has always held that machines have definite limitations. He is prepared to grant that tractors are stronger and faster than oxen, but he feels that they lack experience. "Working cattle were the first helpers that human beings ever had," he said to me, "and so long as there's hard, tricky, hilly, stony work to be done, oxen will be doing it. You'll find people who say that a team of horses or mules can do anything that a yoke of oxen can, but they're mistaken. That's my opinion. I've seen oxen outpull horses and I've got a box of blue ribbons to prove it, and I've seen oxen outthink horses. For one thing, who ever heard of an ox foundering himself? Nobody. But a horse that's real thirsty will keep on drinking water till he topples over. Another thing, and it means a lot to many farmers, is that a yoke costs about ten dollars and a double harness comes to at least seventy-five. Oxen are steadier, too, and they're easier keepers. And when a mule or a horse has to be destroyed, there's nothing to do but bury him. An ox, now, he makes good eating."

"Just what is the difference between a steer and an ox?" I asked.

"I'll tell you what Dad used to say," he replied. "His answer to that always was that it's about the same as the difference between a boy and a man. When a steer gets to be two or three years old, he goes to work and we call him an ox."

Except for a few country gentlemen who have developed a taste for exhibiting mighty oxen at county fairs, most of Mr. Beardsley's customers are New England farmers faced with the necessity of making a living off extremely rough and hilly tracts of land, on which horses, because of their tendency to become excited when the going gets tough, are difficult to maneuver, and on which tractors are impractical because of their tendency to overturn on steep slopes. Mr. Beardsley's best market for his phlegmatic, sure-footed oxen is in the more nearly perpendicular sections of Maine, New Hampshire, and Vermont, and he occasionally sells some in northwestern Connecticut and upstate New York, too. Even farmers in the most rugged regions, though, rarely use oxen for plowing any more; they use them for logging in winter, for clearing fields and hauling stone in the spring and fall, and for hauling hay in summer. Oxen are used to some extent in the swamplands of the deep South because of their willingness to plod, like water buffaloes, through muck so slippery and treacherous that it makes horses nervous. Mr. Beardsley, however, has never tried to sell his oxen in that part of the country; the most distant customer he has ever had is the man in Virginia. He does not advertise his product; the name Beardsley has been so long associated with oxen in the parts of New England where they are used that he feels he can rely on his reputation to bring him his share of whatever business there is. As a raiser of oxen, he has few competitors, and even fewer who make a specialty of one breed, but the number of oxen he sells is not an accurate indication of the number that are being raised nowadays, because farmers who need oxen often raise their own. Mr. Beardsley does not blame them for doing so. He believes that that is a pleasure to which every man is entitled.

When we reached the top of the hill, Mr. Beardsley pulled over to one side of the road and stopped the car. "Well, that's my place," he said, nodding toward the slope of another and even more formidable hill that lay ahead of us across a deep, narrow valley. I could see the road cutting straight up the further hill through tidy green pastures enclosed by zigzag rail fences or low, crumbling stone walls. On one side of the road, about halfway up, was an L-shaped, two-story white clapboard house. It stood in a yard shaded by monumental maples and arthritic old fruit trees and had a wrought-iron fence in front of it. Facing the house, across the road, were two-faded-white barns. A small, ragged cloud floated drowsily above, casting its shadow over one of the steep, immaculate pastures, where a number of rust-colored cattle were grazing.

"Looks pretty, doesn't it?" Mr. Beardsley said. He shook his head in admiration, as though it were he who was seeing it for the first time. "I don't want to brag, as Dad used to say, but it's just about the cleanest farm around here. You couldn't find a stone or a patch of brush on it — haven't been any since my grandfather's time. My great-grandfather cleared as much of it as he could, and Granddad and Dad finished it up. All I've had to do is keep it cleared." He paused and stared reflectively at the panorama. "Granddad died when I was a two-year-old," he said then. "But the funny thing is, I remember him as clear as day. At least, I think I do. It seems to me I can remember sitting on his lap in the kitchen on winter afternoons and watching him whittling out axe handles and yoke pins. He was a husky man and a strong, hard worker. I guess there wasn't much he couldn't do if he put his hand to it. When Granddad got married, his father's house didn't suit him, so he built that house you see there — built it practically all by himself. That was eighty-five years ago, and except for needing some paint, it's as sound now as the day it was built. Granddad hauled every stick of lumber and all the mortar and brick that went into it all the way from New Milford with a wooden-axle cart and three or four pair of good, heavy oxen. Every trip took him the best part of a day. About the most an ox can do is a couple of miles an hour, you know, and New Milford is twelve miles from our place. He used to start out at three o'clock in the morning and he wouldn't get back home with a load until late afternoon. I've been told so many times about how Granddad built our house that I declare I'm beginning to feel like I'd gone along with him every trip." We sat in silence for a moment or two longer, gazing across the valley at the old house and the older land. Then, abruptly, he released the brake and put the car in gear, and we rolled down the hill.

Mr. Beardsley parked the car in the barnyard, and as we got out, he glanced at his watch. "Getting on to eleven," he said. "High time we had a drink. But maybe we'd better take a look around the barns first." I followed him into the larger of the two. On either side of the interior was a long bay filled with hay and at the far end was a row of cattle stalls, empty now, because during the summer Mr. Beardsley turns his stock out to graze. Above the stalls was a high loft, also full of hay. Piled on the floor and hanging from pegs on the wall near the entrance were quantities of wooden yokes and stout drag chains, the equivalent of traces on harness. Most of the yokes were immense things — six or seven feet long and eight or nine inches wide at their thickest point — but I also noticed several that might have been designed for a pair of big dogs. Mr. Beardsley told me that the small ones were used for training calves. "We usually geld our animals at two or three months, and then we start right in breaking them to the yoke," he said. "Naturally, it's a sight easier to start them young than wait until they're full-grown steers and weigh a couple of thousand pounds apiece. If you do it right, you can get a pair pretty well broke in a week or so. Once you've got a pair broke properly, a child can handle them. As a matter of fact, Dad had me driving a good-sized pair before I was six years old. That's the way I had my fun when I was a youngster — hitching up a pair of oxen and driving them all over the place. I guess about the first words I learned to say were 'gee,' 'haw,' and 'whoa.' "

Skirting a massive, flat wooden stoneboat, or sledge, which Mr. Beardsley said was used for hauling stone and timber, preferably when there was snow on the ground but often when there wasn't, we walked down toward the stalls. When we got there, he stepped up on a box in front of a stall and pulled out a handful of hay from the loft. "Here's something I doubt if you ever saw before," he said, holding it out to me. I stared at the stuff, which looked like any hay to me, and then at him. I wondered whether this was some kind of rustic joke, but he seemed to be in dead earnest. "What is it?" I asked. "Well, sir," he replied, "I'd say it was probably the oldest hay in this part of the country — maybe in the whole country. It's seventy-four years old. Granddad cut it with a pair of oxen in the month of June, 1872. I've got a little better than half a ton of it up there. They say hay is like liquor — the older it is, the better. By golly, I'd pay a hundred dollars a ton for hay before I'd feed out any of this. I get a lot of satisfaction out of just having it around." Mr. Beardsley sniffed it, smiled gently, and carefully put it back in the loft. "I guess I feel almost the same way about a cord of wood in the shed out back of the house," he said. "I cut that wood myself when I was nine years old, and I'd hate like everything to have to burn a stick of it. Well, anyway . . ." He hopped off the box, walked over to a door just beyond the stalls, and swung it open, In a matter-of-fact voice, he said, "If you want to see a nice pair of Devons, there you are."

Outside the door was a short ramp that led down to a corral. Two hefty oxen were standing side by side in the middle of the enclosure, switching their tails in unison. They regarded us heavily. Each animal had horns with a spread of at least three feet, the points tipped with blunt brass caps. The horn caps are largely a matter of decoration, Mr. Beardsley explained, since, as a rule, oxen are not much more ferocious than rabbits. "It takes a lot of time and trouble to get a pair matched up as pretty as those are," Mr. Beardsley said. "Even when nature matches a pair up for size, weight, and length of leg, one of them, as like as not, will grow up with more curve to his horns than the other." He went on to say that a patient breeder will attach lead weights to the horns of a calf if they show signs of getting out of line and in this way gradually modify their curve.

We returned to the barnyard, where Mr. Beardsley took another thirsty look at his watch and then said, without much enthusiasm, "Would you be interested in seeing the frame we use for shoeing our animals?" I replied that I would, and he sighed. "Well, it won't take long," he said hopefully, opening the door of the other barn. I said I didn't know that oxen had to be shod. "The truth is, we don't do it much any more," he said, "because we move our animals by truck these days instead of walking them on the road. About the only time we shoe them now is when they're going to work on a rough piece of land where they can use some extra traction. I don't look forward much to a shoeing job. An ox can be a handful when he's being shod. Especially the first time. Some of them thrash around like they'd gone crazy. Also, cattle have split hoofs, you know, and that means eight shoes for every animal. I hate to say it, but when I'm shoeing an ox, I sometimes get to wishing that Beardsleys had been horse breeders." There was a pile of iron shoes on the floor in a corner of the barn, and Mr. Beardsley picked up one of them. It was thin, flat, and kidney-shaped, with a sharp cleat at each end. He handed it to me, saying, "Keep it for a souvenir, if you like. I guess I've got enough shoes around here to outfit half the working cattle in New England. Some of them go back as far as my great-grandfather's time. Not that one, of course. I've got his put away."

The shoeing frame turned out to be a kind of stall, a battered but stout-looking contrivance made of four-by-fours. Mr. Beardsley called my attention first to a yoke whose ends were built into the sides of the frame, and then to a broad leather sling, also suspended from the sides. "Well," he said, "it works like this. That yoke holds the animal's head so he can't back out. The sling fits under his belly. We lower it to let him into the frame and then, when we get it drawed up tight, it keeps him from moving around and also acts as a support for him. Then we strap one of his legs to a board, like a splint, and go to work on it. Our forge is over there in the corner. I don't know about you, but I'm ready for some cider."

I said I was ready, and he led me out of the barn at a brisk clip. We crossed the road and went up a walk to the house. A spotted sow was sprawled under an apple tree in the yard, and four tiny shoats were bounding around her like puppies. Most of the windows in the house were closed and shuttered, but the door toward which we were heading was open. A pair of overshoes stood on the doorstep. "You won't find any frills here," Mr. Beardsley warned me pleasantly. "My mother died back in 1919, and now that Dad's gone, there's just me and Arthur Jones and Cap Goodwin. They've both been working for us almost ever since I can remember. Art's seventy-eight and Cap is seventy-three. You'll meet them at dinner, or maybe before, if they get thirsty. We keep bachelors' hall and we take things pretty easy." Although Mr. Beardsley has never married, he is not, I gathered, a misogamist. The fact is that his life has always been so rich in contentment that he has just never got around to bothering about a wife.

Mr. Beardsley led the way into the kitchen, a large and cheerful room with whitewashed plaster walls and a bare, worn plank floor. (His parlor is stiff, gloomy, and comfortless, and he rarely goes in it, except when he has another hat to add to his collection.) The kitchen contained several straightbacked chairs, two tables, a sagging couch covered with a rug, and a low, square, woodburning cookstove. They all looked as though they had been there for half a century. The stove stood in front of a big fireplace, which was apparently not used, for it was stacked with stove wood. An old Seth Thomas mantel clock in a handsome walnut case stood on a shelf above one of the tables. Near it, on the wall, was a calendar stripped down to the month of May, which was illustrated by a Currier & Ives print of a man driving a yoke of oxen along a road. As Mr. Beardsley passed the stove, he gave it an affectionate pat, as he might a favorite dog. "Here's a stove that Dad gave four dollars for secondhand fifty-five years ago," he said, "and I don't expect to live to see the day when it's worn out."

Turning, he reached up and put his hat on one of six iron hooks that hung down almost a foot from the ceiling. "Those hooks used to support a wooden platform that my grandmother stored food on," he said, "but they've always been just hatracks in my time. It used to be the custom of the house that a man had to be able to kick his hat off its hook before he could have a drink. Dad finally stopped that a few years before he died. He decided it was getting too hard on our hats." Seeing the incredulous look on my face — the hooks were at least a foot above my head — he laughed heartily. "It's easier to do after you've had a couple of drinks," he said. Still chuckling, he fetched a pitcher and two tumblers off a shelf, and swung open a door. We went through it and down a steep flight of steps to a cellar. "What you might call our drawing room," Mr. Beardsley said, with a wink. Three walls of the room were lined with barrels, twenty-five or thirty of them, piled one on top of another. They were fifty-gallon barrels, he told me, and most of them were full, he assured me happily, of well-aged hard cider. He filled the pitcher at the spigot of one of them. Then he filled the glasses from the pitcher, handed me one, and we drank. The cider was cool, dry, and undeniably invigorating.

"I declare," Mr. Beardsley murmured presently, refilling our glasses, "I certainly was dry." He took a long and evidently satisfying swallow and relaxed against the side of a barrel. "This cider of ours has a lot of gumption, you know," he said. "Close to twelve per cent. We age it in old whiskey barrels to give it taste. There've been years when we've had cider that was hard to tell from liquor."

Steps sounded on the floor overhead. "That must be Art and Cap," Mr. Beardsley said. He ran some more cider into the pitcher and we went back upstairs. Two old men in baggy work clothes were sitting in the kitchen, their hands folded primly in their laps. They kept their eyes on Mr. Beardsley's pitcher as he introduced me. Art Jones, a small, spry, dried-up fellow, was wearing a pair of dazzling yellow suspenders, and his hair was slicked down in the roach style that was favored by sporting bartenders back in the McKinley administration. Cap Goodwin, a huge, muscular man with a white, patriarchal beard, struck me as being bald, until I realized that his skull was shaven. "Hot out today," Mr. Jones said to Mr. Beardsley in an amiable chirp. "Cool down cellar, though, eh, Perse?" Mr. Goodwin rumbled softly with amusement at this, and Mr. Beardsley nodded but did not reply. It must have been an old joke. Mr. Beardsley got a bottle of bourbon and some more glasses from a wall cupboard. He poured out four sizable shots of whiskey and four tumblers of cider on the side. The two old men watched every move he made. As he handed the drinks around, he said to me, "Some people like to chase their liquor with beer or water, but we've got in the habit of using cider. Always had plenty of it on hand. I guess that's why." Mr. Jones and Mr. Goodwin began to drink their whiskey with evident enthusiasm. I offered Mr. Beardsley a cigarette. He shook his head and tossed off his bourbon, following it with a swallow of cider. "I don't smoke, chew, gamble, or use profane language," he said. "I'm like Dad that way. He always figured those things got in the way of drinking. The Beardsley's have always got a lot of pleasure out of liquor. A fellow asked Dad one time if he was a hard drinker. 'Nope,' Dad told him. 'It's about the easiest thing I do.' "

Mr. Jones cackled. "Yep," he said. "Nate was quite a man." He turned to me. "Perse's dad was a little fellow, like me, you know, but he never let up. He was a hard worker, and I never heard a bigger talker. Along with everything else, he got himself elected into the state legislature back in 1911. The Democrats was his party. I mind one time when the legislature was meeting, Nate got up and mowed three acres of hay before breakfast. Then he drove his buggy over to Woodbury. Then he took the trolley to Waterbury. Then he rode the train to Hartford and walked up to the Statehouse in time for the meeting. Came home the same way that night. Nate was a man to drive himself hard. He wouldn't let anybody outdo him. Another time, he heard P. T. Barnum was showing off a forty-horse hitch. That gave him an idea. He and us rigged up a forty-ox hitch and we drove it over to the fair at Berlin. Everybody's eyes sure popped out that day. You remember that, Perse?"

"I remember it," Mr. Beardsley said. "That was one thing about Dad, he just couldn't stand to be outdone."

"Nate like to killed me once," Mr. Goodwin said agreeably.

His companions laughed, and Mr. Beardsley said, "That was when everybody was saying what a strong man Cap, here, was. Dad wanted to play a joke on Cap. We'd just got a load of cider and it was still on the wagon — about half a dozen fifty-gallon barrels. A full barrel weighs right around five hundred pounds, and they were all full but one. That one only had ten or fifteen gallons in it. Dad was the only one here who knew it wasn't filled, and he had that barrel spotted. Well, he and Cap were getting ready to unload the wagon, and Dad said, sort of offhand, 'I'll take the first one, Cap, and you take the next.' Cap must have thought Dad had gone crazy, but when he saw him take a barrel off without much trouble, he figured if a little fellow like Dad could do it, he could, too. And, by golly, he did. Cap got under a full barrel and worked with it until he'd eased it down to the ground. About laid you out, though, didn't it, Cap?"

Mr. Goodwin nodded contentedly. "Handled a good many barrels of cider since then," he said, "but only a glass at a time." Then, pointing to the illustrated calendar, he said, "You know, Perse, I've been sitting here thinking that I'll be glad when this month is over, so I won't have to look at that darned picture any more." I asked him why he didn't like it, and he looked mildly astonished. "Why, that fool artist's got the driver walking on the off side of his team," he said. "You'd think even an artist would have sense enough to know you've got to walk on the near side to drive a yoke of oxen." He pulled thoughtfully at his beard. "That picture does put me in mind, though, of the old days when we used to walk the fair circuit," he continued. "Nate, Perse, Art, and me — we used to make them all. Berlin, Wolcott, Goshen, Charter Oak, West Hartford, Middlebury, Huntington, New Milford, Riverton, Danbury, and even Mt. Kisco, over in York State — some of them fairs nobody ever heard of these days. We'd start out one morning late in September or early October with the cattle we were showing that year, and sometimes we wouldn't get home for near a month. Took us a full day to walk our cattle twenty miles. When we went to Mt. Kisco — that's maybe fifty miles from here — we'd be three days on the road. Nights, we'd put up at some farm along the way. They'd be glad to see us and we'd get to bed late. But old Nate, he'd have us back on the road about sunup."

"A vacation with work," piped Mr. Jones. "That's what I used to call fair time. Work all day showing cattle and collecting ribbons and prize money, drink liquor and watch the hootchy-kootchy girls all evening, and then sleep rolled up in a blanket in a corner of a barn. Be mornings when we'd wake up and our blankets were frozen stiff as a board from the cold."

We all sat without talking for a few moments. Presently, Mr. Beardsley got up and opened a door to a storeroom in which I could see some hams and pork shoulders hanging on a rack, several cases of beer, and a barrel heaped full of hazelnuts. He rummaged around in it for a while and then came back with a crusty stone quart bottle. "Before I start getting dinner ready," he told me, "I want you to taste some real old apple brandy. My Uncle Jhiel Beardsley bought this bottle in a saloon sixty-five years ago. Lord knows how old the stuff was then." He poured a few drops into a glass and handed it to me. The brandy was almost colorless and it was as bland as tea. Mr. Beardsley, Mr. Jones, and Mr. Goodwin watched me closely as I drank. I said it was gentle and very fine. "It's a real treat," Mr. Beardsley said. Mr. Jones caught my eye and winked. "Kind of small for its age, though, ain't it, son?" he said.

The Pleasure and the Art

I drove out to the hamlet of Silverbrook, a roadside eruption in the pine barrens of northeastern Long Island, one February morning, and passed a convivial afternoon at the Silverbrook Art Glass Works. Silverbrook is about two miles south of Riverhead, the seat of Suffolk County; it takes its name from a tarnished tidewater creek that seeps down through the surrounding thickets to a nearby inlet of the Great Peconic Bay; and it has a population of around forty. There is a huddle of summer cottages on the beach and there are others buried in the brush, but most of the settlement — a liquor store, a bait stand, a bakery, a hardware store, a tavern, a couple of grocery stores, two lunchrooms, a juke-box café, eight or ten shiny little houses, and four ramshackle filling stations — straggles along several hundred yards of Route 24, the main cross-island highway in those parts. The Silverbrook Art Glass Works factory sits in a ragged fifty-foot clearing behind a lunchroom called Mary Ann's Place. It is a one-story cube of cinder blocks, painted gray, with a battlemented false front and a broad, double-doored entrance, and it looks like a seedy garage. A sandy lane, indicated by an inconspicuous arrow sign and peppered with broken glass, wanders up to the building from the highway. The business was established in 1945 by three brothers named Kreutz, and they operate it almost entirely themselves. Their only employees are a handyman and a woman shipping-clerk-and-typist. Two of the brothers, Henry and Frank, are in their early forties, and bachelors. The other, Joseph, is forty-eight and married, and has two young sons. The Kreutzes are natives of Lednické Rovne, in Czechoslovakia, and members of a family whose men for at least four generations have been glass-blowers. They came to the United States in 1943, they all live together in a comfortable bungalow not far from the factory, and they are deeply devoted to each other, to hunting and fishing and beer, and to the unhurried creation of elegant, handmade Bohemian-glass tableware.

There was snow in the air on the day of my visit, and a bitter wind blowing. I reached Mary Ann's Place around noon, cold to the bone, and went in and had a bowl of soup and a sandwich. Then, thawed but not warmed, I headed up the lane to the factory. The glassy sand squeaked and crunched under my heels like ice. A haze of smoke or steam hung over the building, and a gold light glowed through the windows. One of the big doors was ajar. On the threshold stood a short, thickset, red-cheeked man, gazing peacefully at the soggy sky. His hair was matted with sweat, he was stripped down to his undershirt, and he had a can of beer in his hand. My teeth began to chatter. He raised his beer can in a cheerful salute. I went up to him and introduced myself. "So?" he said amiably, and took a long swallow of beer. "Always here visitors are welcome. Is a pleasure for us." He shook the can and drank again, and then tossed it into the brush. "Also, is now a good time to talk to Joe. We are resting after lunch. He is head from the partners — Joe. I am Frank Kreutz, the middle one. Come."

Mr. Kreutz heaved back the door. A spine-tingling blast of hot air rolled out and over us. I followed him into a gritty, gray-walled chamber that extended the width and almost the length of the building. In the middle of the floor stood a lumpy brick furnace about the size of a depot stove, with its door open and a darting fang of flame. Facing it was a charred workbench strewn with tools and empty beer cans and forgotten cigarette stubs. Shelves and sawhorse tables piled with dusty glassware lined two walls, and there was a jumble of barrels and packing boxes, a grindstone, and a commodious sink along a third. At the far end of the room, near a dim archway, two men were moving darkly about against the blazing mouth of another, and enormous, brick furnace. It was head-high, six feet wide, and easily nine feet long, and it was panting like a locomotive. Mr. Kreutz paused just inside the door and waved a hospitable hand. "Be at home," he said. "Inspect the samples. I will tell Joe." I nodded as he turned away, but it was a moment before I knew what he had said. After the cold and damp, the sudden heat was stupefying. My overcoat felt as heavy as stone, and it was all I could do to unbutton it. Even the roof of my mouth was hot. There was a thermometer on the wall nearby. It was the only thing in the place that interested me just then, and I made an effort and went over and looked at it. It read ninety-three.

When I had shed my overcoat and jacket and loosened my necktie, I began to feel better. I found a chair in a corner under a half-open window and sat down. On the window sill lay a dribble of melted snow. I was rolling up my sleeves when Joseph Kreutz approached. He is a wiry, bespectacled man of medium height, with lank, thinning hair, an abrupt but gentle smile, and an air of subdued excitement. He was wearing loose moccasins, green duck trousers, and a sooty short-sleeved jersey, and he hadn't shaved for several days. "How do you do?" he said, giving me a long look and a fleeting handshake. "But already, I see, you have made yourself comfortable. Good. I am sorry for the heat today. It is more hot than usual."

"Why is that?" I asked.

"The reason is the wind," Mr. Kreutz said. "When there is much wind, like now, and from the northeast, we cannot long leave open the doors. It cools too quick the glass. So today we suffer a little bit. Be thankful, though, you have not come in summer. Then, with all open doors and windows and the ovens turned low as possible if we are to go on working, the temperature is still one hundred twenty degrees at least, Fahrenheit. Sometimes one hundred fifty. I say that only so you will feel more cool. Such heat is too much even for us. Unless there is a fast order, nothing is doing here in summer — in July and August — except now and then in the nighttime. We are always fishing." He raised a finger. "One moment . . ."

Mr. Kreutz hurried away across the room. He returned with two misted cans of beer, handed me one, and dropped contentedly into a chair at my side. "Now we are ready to talk," he said. "I have arranged for the time. Later, when there is work to do, you can stand and watch and see how beautiful glass is made. Do you drink from the can? Good. Then — *prosit!*" We lifted our cans and drank, and at the first swallow I was seized with a bottomless thirst. It was almost embarrassing. I had gulped half the can before I could stop. "For us," Mr. Kreutz went on, lighting a cigarette, "the glass is too much trouble. Naturally, everything in that line is here — mugs, flutes, steins, we make them all — but we cannot be bothered to pour. We drink while we work. I will explain. All here enjoy beer. Why deny it? But we are not drunkards. Liquids are necessary at this heat, and beer is best. Water is a danger. I do not know why. I know only — drink water and you are all of a sudden sick and bloated, without strength. Beer escapes in sweat. In five minutes, the beer is out. Already now you are sweating. I drink every day at work ten, twelve, sometimes twenty cans, and never feel it. Right away, it is out. I would not drink it otherwise. Wine is the same. In South America, where we came first from Czechoslovakia, we drank the wine. Glassmakers must drink and the beer there was no good. The American beer is O.K., pretty good. We can drink it. It is not, of course, Pilsner."

Mr. Kreutz refreshed himself and smiled. "No." he said. "But why do I talk of beer? We are not a brewery. Frank says you are interested in glass. What an invention! Nothing in the world is like it. Always people are thinking of glass, Look out, it will break. They think only of the one trouble with glass. It has no other. Think what else is glass. I will name them. It is easy to work — more easy than wood. Any shape is possible. It is cheap — nothing costs less. Except it is brittle, it cannot be destroyed. Glass will not rust or corrode or rot or burn, and even acids are harmless. It has luster like a jewel. Also, like nothing else, it is transparent. I say this because I know about glass in every way. I am a glassblower from the age of fourteen. At seven or eight, I started learning. My brothers, of course, are the same. It was in the blood from our father and grandfather and great-grandfather and maybe before. Once, like us, our great-grandfather had his own factory. But I am also a designer. Everything here is not only offhand — no molds — but original, by my own ideas. The glass, too, we make ourselves. In back there, through the archway, is the mixing room. The formula is mine. When I was fourteen, I could make something from glass, but that was not enough. I told my father, 'I want the chemistry. I wish to make glass, not only blow. I must know how come the glass.' He said, 'Joe, wait a few years. Keep blowing.' He was right. At twenty, through his friends, I started in the glass-industry school — the best — in Haida. The school was six years, and after that an examination and a diploma. But I had learned much while working, so I was in the school six months only when I was ready for the examination and received the diploma. In Europe, the diploma is everything. Soon I was manager of the mixing room and the glass-blowing room at the firm Joseph Inwald, in Prague. I was there eleven years, to 1937. Next I was manager of Fábrica Nacional de Vidrios, in La Paz, Bolivia."

"How did you happen to leave Europe?" I asked.

"Why," Mr. Kreutz replied, raising his eyebrows, "there was war coming. Even then, in 1937, anyone could see it. I said to my wife and Frank and Henry, my close brothers, 'Time to go.' My father was lost in the other war, and we were fourteen children at home. That was enough lesson. I did not wish to die for the Fatherland. I prefer to live, you know. We four went first to Bolivia because of a friend there in glass. After that, we were five years in Montevideo, Uruguay. Then, in 1943, we took the chance and came to this country. Everyone hopes for America. Besides, in Montevideo we were making mostly window glass. We had no trouble here. There was always work for the expert men. We were working different places — Bethpage, on Long Island; the town of Tiffin, Ohio; and in Brooklyn — for two years to learn the customs. For example, I had then a big mustache. Now, no more. It was not American. I noticed all the customs. I learned there is no popularity for the colored glass. A good thing. Colored glass I can make in twenty-six colors, but to me it is not beautiful. Color can hide cheapness. Give me for nothing colored-glass anything and I won't take it. I like best the nice, clear glass — plain, no cutting or engraving. Also, we saved our money. I told my brothers, 'We will start soon for ourself. There was no reason here to work always for others. We have too much art. You understand, wherever we worked, even at the U.S. Glass Company, in Tiffin — a very good shop — always the other men were looking at us. To them it was a mystery how we could make from glass so easy whatever was wanted. In the American factory, almost all, it is specialization and the assembly line. One man can make only tumblers, maybe, another only bowls, some only a little part. They are like boys or old, old men. And molds — always they must have a mold. In this country, I think, you can count on the fingers of your hands the glass-blowers who can make good work by offhand. Of course, the mold is quicker and for some things O.K. But where is the pleasure and the art?"

Mr. Kreutz finished his beer. Then he caught up my can, which had been empty for ten minutes or more, and fetched another restorative round. As I watched him, I realized that I had almost forgotten the heat. I felt relaxed but no longer limp. And this time I drank less greedily. I was still thirsty and the cold beer tasted even better than before, but I could sip it now. After a moment, I asked Mr. Kreutz why he and his brothers had chosen to settle in eastern Long Island. "Was it because there's so much sand around here?" I added.

"Ah," he said. "Always people are wondering. Always thinking that. The reason is we are sportsmen. Here on Long Island is good shooting — ducks and geese and even pheasant — and, of course, much fishing. The best. One can make glass anyplace, but not everywhere is good sport. I like this work, you know. It is like play for me, and a good living. But who wants to be a millionaire always working? Life is to enjoy. So? Our way is fishing and hunting. That is the whole reason we are here. The beach sand is no good. It has too much of iron oxide and aluminum. It comes green when melted, like the edge of window glass. Our sand is from Pennsylvania. None is better. It is white like snow — ninety-nine-per-cent pure silica. In Europe, the sand is only seventy-two per cent. The chemistry is more important there. When the sand is pure, the expert glassmaker has no trouble. Anyone can make it, almost. There is necessary only the sand, a little potash or soda for alkali, lime for base, some small proportions of certain chemicals to make perfect, the whiteness, and much heat. The best is Bohemian glass, like here. No glass has less color and none is so hard. It is as hard as hard. For glass, it is iron. I will show you."

Mr. Kreutz plucked a pudgy tumbler from the nearest table of samples. "A regular item," he said, resuming his seat. "Eighteen dollars a dozen, retail. But watch!" Holding the glass by the rim, he struck it smartly against a leg of his chair. Nothing happened. Then he struck it again, much harder, and again. At the fourth whack, it broke, just below the rim, and the bottom shattered on the concrete floor. "Now you know for yourself," he said cheerfully, and dropped the remaining fragment among the wreckage. "Tough stuff, eh?" I said I hadn't supposed even crystal was that strong. Mr. Kreutz looked at me. "Excuse me," he said. "There is no strength in crystal glass. Crystal is the supreme art glass — something special — but also the most brittle. The base of crystal glass is lead, not lime. From lead comes heaviness and tone like a bell and a beautiful luster, but its nature is weakness. Bohemian glass is merely the most beautiful of hard glass. My hope, naturally, is someday here to make crystal glass. I have the chemistry. The trouble is the cost. Lead is not cheap." He smiled. "Some think now our glass is crystal. Not only customers. Last year, our brother John, who works with glass in Buenos Aires, wished to see our work, so we sent him a few samples. Poor John! It cost him money. They would not believe at the customhouse our work was only glass. He must pay the heavy import duty for crystal. Of course, it was our best. All art work. When there is more money here, we will be a crystal shop. I will make a crystal as good as Steuben, even. Perhaps better. I do not apologize for our glass, you understand. But it is a fact we are best now only in design."

A tall, fair-haired young woman in slacks and a tight jersey emerged from the back room. Under her arm was a bulky record book. She spread it open on one of the tables in the midst of a battalion of cocktail shakers and began to leaf through it. "Ah," Mr. Kreutz said, touching my arm. "Here is Doris Austria. Her husband, Frank, is our helper. I wish you to know her. Come." He led me rapidly down the room, and Mrs. Austria, closing her book on a pencil, received us with a solemn smile. She said she was pleased to meet me. "He is learning about glass," Mr. Kreutz said. Then he turned to me. "Doris alone is the office here," he said. "What would we do without her!"

Mrs. Austria gave a little laugh. "Well, I'll say this," she said. "I never worked in a nicer place."

"No," Mr. Kreutz said. "But I am telling the truth. Until Doris came, a year ago, there were terrible times. Every letter was a torture. I can write in Czech, of course, and German, and in Bohemian and Hungarian and Spanish, but not yet in English. I would spend an hour, often two, to answer one customer's letter. I had a table of dictionaries — all kinds, many languages. Now there is no more trouble. Doris does it all. I do not know even the names of who buys our glass."

"Well, I don't either," Mrs. Austria said. "Not all of them. We ship glass to forty-three different states and all the big stores. You know — Lord & Taylor, Abercrombie & Fitch, John Wanamaker, Marshall Field, and like that."

"I know John Wanamaker," Mr. Kreutz said. "He was the first to buy — "

"There's the phone," Mrs. Austria said with annoyance, cocking her head toward a distant tinkle. She lunged around me, and away.

"She is a necessity — Doris," Mr. Kreutz said. "Like beer. But I was saying about John Wanamaker. We were not doing so good before he saw Silverbrook Glass. It is easy in this country to start a business, more easy than Europe, but it is easy also to be finished. When the war was over, art glass was the first item the people gave up buying. So hard times came, but I would not stop. I told my brothers, 'I stay here if I eat only one

time a day.' For two years I said that, and then all of
a sudden we were safe. An idea came to me — the flame
design! It gave us life. Do you know that style?"

I said I didn't think so. "I'd like to see it," I added.

"Gladly," he said. "This way. But first . . ." He
stopped before a shelf holding an assortment of handsome cylindrical flasks and vases, gnarled bowls, and
potbellied pitchers, and several figurines of frisking fish,
and pheasants poised for flight. He directed my attention to the figurines. They looked as if they had been
carved out of ice. "Here is special art work," he said,
caressing a fragile fin. "Twenty-eight dollars a pair and
up, retail. Notice how real. Almost like life. Naturally.
They are made by sportsmen. In five years here, no one
has copied our figures. They try, but they cannot make
like us. It is the same with the flame design. Imitators!
To me they are a puzzle. I would be ashamed." Mr.
Kreutz shook his head and moved on to a honeycomb
of glasses. There were forty or fifty of them — liqueur
glasses, shot glasses, cocktail glasses, highball glasses,
beer flutes, and foot-tall julep glasses, and others, big
and little and in between, of ambiguous function. The
flanks of some were as plain as jelly jars and some were
delicately crackled, but most were decorated here and
there with tiny, twisted, flamelike ridges. I picked up one
of the last, an Old-Fashioned glass that would hold at
least a pint. Its little tongues of flame fitted snugly
against my fingers, its texture was flawless, and its shape,

like that of all offhand glassware, was faintly and agreeably cockeyed. It was a trifle more oval than round and
its rim was just perceptibly undulating. Mr. Kreutz was
silent for a moment, watching me. Then he cleared his
throat and said, "They are beautiful, eh — the little
flames?" I replied that they were indeed. "Yes," he continued. "I would say the same no matter who was the
maker. Not too fancy and not too plain. Only someone
who knows fire would have such an idea. You wonder
maybe how the flame is made. So? Well, now it is time
for me to work a little and you will see that, and more."

We cut across the rear of the room toward the big furnace. Through the archway, I caught a glimpse of somebody shoveling a pile of broken glass into a barrel. The
temperature seemed to rise at every step we took. Frank
Kreutz and another man, taller and thicker and ruddier,
were lounging on a box near the furnace, companion-
ably drinking beer and smoking. They were dripping
wet, but they looked at peace with the world. As we approached, they lazily stood up. Joseph introduced me
to the big man. "My brother Henry," he said. "Frank
already you know." He gazed at them with satisfaction.
"We are a team. Frank begins. Henry shapes. And I am
the finisher. That is our habit only. All, of course, are
experts. The molten glass is here in this furnace — the
fusing oven, we call it. It is automatic oil-fired and in it
the glass is made. We make four thousand pounds —

enough supply for two days — three times a week, at night. In the daytime, we cannot spare the time. To mix glass properly, even by cement mixer, takes three hours, and fusing, in the oven, sixteen more. Here is something to know. The best glass is made with a little broken old glass added. The fusing comes quicker that way. A blessing. Otherwise there would be terrible waste from breakage in a glass factory. Also — Wait!" I had taken a step toward the furnace. I stopped and glanced at him. "If you were going to look in the door, don't," he said. "The temperature inside is twenty-four hundred degrees, Fahrenheit. Maybe twenty-five. That is too hot and bright for the eyes."

While we were talking, Frank had drifted around behind the furnace. He came back carrying a blowpipe, a slender iron tube about the length of a broomstick, with a brass mouthpiece at one end and a small knob at the other. Henry grinned and said something to him in what I took to be Czech. They both looked inquiringly at Joseph. "I think a few decanters," he said. "Little bottles, with the flame. O.K.?" Henry shrugged and tossed off the last of his beer. Frank walked over to the furnace. Averting his eyes from the glare of shimmering light, he gripped the blowpipe with both hands and poked it slowly through the door. I watched him, squinting. For an instant, he held the pipe motionless. Then, with a spinning thrust, he sank it deep into the heart of the oven. "When the pipe is cold," Joseph told me, tapping a cigarette on his wrist, "the glass won't stick. So first the tip must be heated. Now he is taking glass." As he spoke, Frank backed away from the door, pulling the pipe out. He headed for a low iron-topped worktable, holding the pipe with the tip slightly raised and twirling it rapidly. Clinging to the tip was a dab of brilliant orange, like a kumquat. When he reached the table, he lowered the pipe and rolled the tip of it back and forth across the iron top, shaping the viscid glass into a firm cylinder. Then he raised the mouthpiece to his lips and gently exhaled. The cylinder quivered, paled, and abruptly rounded into a bubble the size of a golf ball. He gave the pipe a final spin and held it out toward Joseph, who leaned forward and touched his cigarette alight on the hot glass. Then Frank handed the pipe to Henry. With a grunt, Frank dropped back on the box and picked up his beer, and Henry made for the furnace. He plunged the pipe through the door, and down and around. When he withdrew it, the bubble had vanished. In its place hung a trembling, fistlike gob. Joseph laid a friendly hand on my shoulder. "Always the beginning is the same," he said. "It makes no difference what item. First comes the little bubble. That is all the glass the empty pipe will take. But such a little bit, of course, is not enough for working. So Henry must get more glass to make bigger the bubble. As you see. How much he takes depends on what we are making." Henry passed us at a shuffling trot, holding the pipe to his mouth with its stem revolving and a bright new bubble, a trifle larger than a baseball, ballooning at the tip. Suddenly he stopped dead and with both hands swung the pipe in a violent downward arc — and the bubble was transformed into a plump and pendulous teardrop. Then, clapping the mouthpiece briefly to his lips again, he moved on. "Gravity does it," Joseph said as we turned to follow him. "And centrifugal force. To the expert, it is more sure than the mold." Henry halted at the workbench. In the middle of it was rooted an old oarlock. With one hand, he eased the pipe into the oarlock, and with the other rummaged through the litter on the bench until he found a charred, paddle-shaped shingle. With a twist of the pipe and a slap of the shingle, he flattened the end of the drop. It was beginning to look like a bottle. Then he exchanged the paddle for a pair of tweezers, and pinched out eight or ten spirals of flame around the belly of the bottle. I watched him with a sense of disappointment. It was hard to believe that those effortless plucks could baffle even the least gifted imitator. Joseph noticed my expression, and smiled faintly. "When somebody knows something, it is very easy," he said. Henry chuckled.

Taking the pipe from Henry, Joseph went on, "Now comes the finishing. The neck must be shaped, and the lip. Also, other things. But for such work the pipe is in the way. I cannot make the neck and lip with the pipe in such position. It must be changed. Here is Frank to

help. So watch." Frank sauntered up from the furnace
swinging another blowpipe tipped with a minute smear
of hot glass. He stationed himself on the other side of
the bench, facing his brother. Then, simultaneously, Joseph thrust his pipe across the bench and Frank stabbed
the tip of his hard against the base of the bottle. When
the new glass had congealed and the bottle was firmly
joined to Frank's pipe, Joseph picked up a triangular
file and dipped it into a pail of water at his feet. He
tapped the neck of the bottle with the wet file. The glass
broke instantly and evenly away from Joseph's pipe, as
though he had slashed it with a diamond. He smiled another faint smile. "A little trick," he explained, ex-
changing pipes with Frank. "It is like the flame. When
you know, it is very easy. I am talking in fun, of course.
But also so you will understand that with glass every
touch must be sure. One little mistake and all must start
all over again." He stepped to the small furnace. "For
the finishing, now, more heat is necessary. The glass is
getting cold and stiff. See how in places it is coming
black? If I wait too long — boom! It will explode. The
reason is, different temperatures inside the glass and
out. So this little furnace is here for reheating. The
other, naturally, is too hot." He edged the bottle through
the door and screwed it deep into the thicket of fire.
"Glass must cool slowly," he said, glancing now at me
and now at the reddening bottle. "We have for that a
cooling oven. The annealing oven is the name. It is in

back, and there goes all finished items. It is not hot —
only six hundred degrees, Fahrenheit — but enough for
safety. At the end of work, automatically the temperature goes slowly down. After eighteen hours, the glass is
ready to polish and sell. Sometimes, in early morning,
when the temperature is no more than maybe one hundred twenty degrees, one of us will crawl inside for a
little sweat. That way we keep well. Also, inside we
cook — fish and game and even a whole pig. It is better
than any stove. Such food no one has ever tasted. See
the big pair tweezers there on the bench — will you hand
them, please? *Děkuju*."

He drew out the bottle with a movement that set it
spinning, closed the tweezers on its neck, and gave a
gentle tug. The soft glass pulled like taffy. The neck
lengthened, and the lip trembled and flared and flattened. Then he rammed the tweezers down the neck,
probed the belly for a moment, wrenched them out, and
held the completed bottle aloft. "So!" he said. I felt like
applauding.

There was a crunching footstep behind us. It was
Frank. He took the pipe from his brother and carried
the bottle off to the cooling oven. Joseph mopped his
brow. "Time for beer," he remarked, and went to fetch
some. When he returned, Henry had another bottle
ready for finishing and Frank was strolling punctually
around the end of the bench to help in the exchange of
pipes. Joseph handed me a can of beer, took a hurried

gulp from his own, and deposited it on the bench. "No more talk," he said cheerfully. "We are started now and all must go fast to keep up. You understand and excuse? Of course. It is for a few minutes only. Maybe half an hour. Then we will have a little to eat. There are potatoes to roast in the oven, and also a beefsteak." He raised his eyebrows and reached for Henry's pipe. I stood by the bench for a moment, and then moved over to the wall and sat down on a crate and sipped my beer, and watched the work from there. It was pleasant work to watch, and presently Frank brought me another beer.

Some Ladies in Retirement

BETWEEN the Revolution and the Civil War, at least a hundred communistic societies were set up in this country. Most of them were of an energetically unorthodox religious character, and all were humble, agrarian, and generally unpopular. Few of them lasted very long. Of the less than a dozen societies that gathered sufficient momentum to survive both the deaths of their founders and the Civil War, only one is still in existence. That is the United Society of Believers in Christ's Second Appearing, the members of which are usually called Shakers.

The United Society was the first American communal organization, and it was always the largest, the richest, and the most austere of the lot. It is composed of celibate men and women, who live under the same roof — though carefully segregated — in more or less self-sufficient groups, or "families," several of which, situated within walking distance of a community meetinghouse, traditionally comprise a "village." Its members abjure pork, alcohol, tobacco, doctors, instrumental music, and architectural and sartorial ornamentation. The theology of the order is, perhaps as much as anything, a chilly derivative of Quakerism and seventeenth-century French millennialism. The sect got its start in England in 1747, during the course of a Quaker revival, but it did not acquire much vitality until nearly a quarter of a century later, when one of its members, a thirty-four-year-old Manchester millworker named Ann Lee, underwent a spiritual experience that gave her such a fervent abhorrence of the weaknesses of the flesh that she was chosen to lead the group. Gradually, the doctrine was evolved that Christ was female as well as male and that He had been reincarnated in Mother Ann, as the leader became known to the believers, thus fulfilling the promise of His Second Coming. In 1774, four years after Mother Ann was selected to head the sect, a revelation persuaded her to lead her eight most loyal followers — six men and two women — to America. They landed at New York, where Mother Ann lived for two years in miserable poverty while her disciples spread out over the countryside, asserting her divinity and proclaiming her belief in a communal life and isolation from world distractions. Mother Ann, who, like her followers, had recurrent trouble with puritanical authorities suspicious of the sect's claim to celibacy, subsequently moved to a farm near Watervliet, New York, where she died in 1784, exhausted by evangelism, privation, and frequent jailings. Shortly thereafter, the United Society of Believers in Christ's Second Appearing was organized. The first Shaker settlement, which was named Mount Lebanon, was established in 1787 about twenty-five miles southeast of Albany, in Columbia County, by Joseph Meacham, one of Mother Ann's original disciples. The society reached its greatest strength during the eighteen-fifties. At that time, it owned well over a hundred thousand acres of fruitful land, had a membership of some five thousand, and maintained eighteen villages, each of which contained at least two large families, in seven states — New York, Maine, New Hampshire, Massachusetts, Connecticut, Ohio, and Kentucky.

Shakerism is moribund now. There have been no converts to it in the past forty years, and since conversion is naturally the sole means of perpetuating a continent order, the membership is rapidly dwindling. Fewer than fifty members are left in the entire society. Only four villages remain — Hancock, in Massachusetts; Canterbury, in New Hampshire; Sabbathday Lake, in Maine; and Mount Lebanon. Mount Lebanon once had eight families, but, like the others, it is now down to one. This, as I found when I drove up there one brilliant summer day, consists of six women and one man. The youngest of them is sixty and the oldest is ninety-two. They live together — lonely, retrospective, and gently backslidden — in a house that was built for a family of seventy-five or more.

Mount Lebanon, despite the implication of its name, is tucked away in a deep pocket in the Berkshires, near the Massachusetts line. A gravel road, cut into the face of a wooded hill, leads down to it from the Albany-Pittsfield highway, which winds through the uplands. I turned into this road a little after noon on the day of my visit, dropped precipitously for a couple of hundred feet, rounded a sharp bend, and came abruptly upon the settlement. It was a subduing sight — a phalanx of seven big, rawboned, white clapboard buildings of indeterminate purpose, all rearing up among towering elms and maples. The largest, a broad, six-story structure, stood within a few feet of the road. The others, some of three stories and some of four, were ranked behind it at the bottom of a slope, symmetrically arrayed in two parallel rows. To one side and at some distance from the large building, was a mammoth gray stone barn, built on the slope, with an upper entrance on the road and another, at the opposite end, leading into a barnyard far below. There was no sound or sight of life, but the six-story building, unlike the others, looked as if it might be occupied. A strip of weedy lawn in front of it had recently been cut, and its windows, though uncurtained and coldly staring, were immaculate. I pulled up in front of it and got out. The house had two identical front doors, about a hundred feet apart. The day was bright and bland, but both were tightly closed. As I hesitated, wondering which door to approach, the one on my left opened a crack, and a woman of advanced but incalculable age, with a dark, wrinkled face, peered out. "I like to see what's going on," she remarked, apparently addressing me. Before I could reply, a voice behind her called, "Now, Sarah, you know you haven't got your wrap." The old woman gave a shrill, mischievous laugh. "I'm as tough as a pine knot," she cried, and vanished, slamming the door.

Then the other door opened and a somewhat younger woman came out. She was short, plump, and pink-and-white, and she wore a long, plain, full-skirted blue dress. I learned later that Shaker women have always worn dresses of this design, which was current in the eighteenth century, in emulation of Mother Ann, who favored it; the clothes of Shaker men have tended to keep more in step with the times. The woman smiled at me with friendly curiosity. I walked over, introduced myself, and asked if I might look around the place. "You're very welcome here," she said. "I hope you didn't mind Sister Sarah Collins. Poor Sarah is ninety-two, and sometimes she acts a little queer. We're always glad to have good people call on us, and I'd enjoy showing you what there is to see." She closed the door and came out on the lawn. "I suppose you know that the North Family, is what we're called, is all that's left of Mount Lebanon. Everything else in the village, even our meetinghouse, has been sold, and most of the buildings have been torn down or moved away. But one Shaker family is a

lot like another. We believe in uniformity. The rest of
the village was on down the road a ways. The reason
we're called the North Family is that we're at the north
end. Shaker families are named for their location. But
I haven't told you *my* name yet. I'm Sister Jennie —
J-e-n-n-i-e — Wells. It isn't J-e-n-n-y, because I'm no
mule." She laughed merrily. "Shakers don't approve of
mules, you know. We've never had any. We think
they're unnatural."

An expression of intense concentration appeared on
Sister Jennie's face. "I'm trying to think where to begin,"
she said. "Most of our visitors these days are antique
collectors, and all they're interested in is buying up what
little fine old handmade Shaker furniture we have left.
Why, those people would grab the chairs right out from
under us if we'd let them. Our furniture is very fashion-
able all of a sudden, you know. I understand it's called
modernistic." She gave me an amused glance. "Maybe
that proves just how far ahead of the world Shakerism
is. We don't make furniture — or anything, for that
matter — now, but when we did, we made it exactly like
the furniture the first Shakers made. We're always being
told how beautiful our things are. I don't say they aren't,
but that isn't what they were meant to be. Shakers aren't
concerned with anything as frivolous as beauty. All our
furniture was ever meant to be was strong, light, plain,
and, above all, practical. It is, too, as you'll see when we
go inside. But I want you to see the rest of the place

first. Then we'll come back here to the dwelling house. That's our name for the house a Shaker family lives in. No matter how large a family got in the old days, and some of them got close to a hundred, it never had more than one dwelling house. When this house was finished, in 1812 or around then, it was four stories, but the family grew so fast that two more had to be added a few years later. Well, that's one problem we don't have to worry about any more. There are only seven of us left in the North Family, and our house has eighty-one rooms."

"How does it happen to have two front doors?" I asked.

"It has two back doors, too," Sister Jennie said. "And also two center halls on every floor. You might say a Shaker dwelling house is really two houses. The men live in the left half and the women in the right. We each have our own parlors, and everything. The only room that we share is the dining room, but we eat at separate tables. Shaker men and women aren't even permitted to shake hands with each other. My stars," she added smiling reproachfully, "I hope you didn't think that we actually *lived* together!"

I assured her that I hadn't, and we started up the road in the direction of a flagstone path that led down between the dwelling house and the barn to the other buildings. After a moment, she said, "I'm sure there's no need for me to point out our barn. You couldn't very

well miss it, could you?" I replied that it was probably
the biggest barn I had ever seen. "I'm sure it is," she said,
beaming. "I don't want to sound vainglorious, but it's
the biggest stone barn in the whole United States. It's
fifty feet wide and it's two hundred and ninety-six feet
long and, as you can see, it has five floors. That's very unusual. It was built in the eighteen-fifties, and it's as
sturdy now as the day it was finished. At that, it's the
newest building in the North Family. The others are
considerably over a hundred years old. The Shakers always built for permanence. We say that Shakerism can't
be told; it must be lived. Still, you can learn a lot about
it just from that barn.

"We're a very practical people," she went on. "There's
no foolishness about anything we do. Our barn was
made the length it is for good reason. The men wanted
to have room enough for a dozen or more loaded wag-
ons on the floor at the road level, in case a sudden storm
came up during haying. That doesn't mean much now,
of course. We don't raise much hay. Our stock is down
to ten milch cows and four horses, which is just a fraction of what we used to have. We've sold or rented out
most of our land, too. The North Family farm was good-
sized once — nearly a thousand acres — but now it's not
much more than two hundred, including pasture and
wood lots, and we have to hire two men to do the work.
About all we're able to do ourselves is housework. But
no matter. Another thing about the barn is that it's

wide enough for a big team and wagon to turn around in. The reason it's built on a slope is so hay can be hauled in at the top floor and pitched *down* to the mows. Then it's pitched *down* from there to the stock stalls below. In most barns, you know, hay has to be pitched *up*. A good many Shaker barns are built like ours. Shakers have never seen any sense in fighting against gravity." Sister Jennie looked at me earnestly. "Not that we mind working hard," she assured me. "We believe in it. Even our elders and eldresses are expected to do their share of manual work. They're our leaders, you know. Every family is supposed to have two elders and two eldresses. We have only one eldress now, and we haven't had an elder in years. Anyway, as I was saying, there aren't any loafers in a Shaker family. Loafing and communism just don't go together. Mother Ann said, 'Hands to work and hearts to God,' and that's our guiding rule. I wish you could have come to see us forty or fifty years ago. A Shaker farm was a busy place in those days."

As we walked down the path, I asked Sister Jennie how long she had been a Shaker. "Practically all my life," she said, with satisfaction. "I'm seventy years old, although I may not look it and I certainly don't feel it, and the Groveland Shakers, up near Rochester, took me in when I was just four. I was a half orphan, with a cruel stepfather, and my mother thought I'd be better off with the Shakers. Back in those days, you know, there weren't many good orphan asylums. The Shakers occasionally adopted poorly situated children or children who had no parents, and educated and looked after them until they became of age. Every Shaker family had its own school, and they were very good. They had to be. We don't admire ignorance. When a Shaker child was twenty-one, he was free either to go out into the world or stay and be gathered into the Church as a convert. Four of us here at Mount Lebanon came to Shakerism as children. That's merely a coincidence, though. Most Shakers have been converted from the world. We've converted Jews, atheists, and all kinds of Protestants — everything but Catholics. There were still a few converts coming in when I was a girl, before the world got too strong for us. I must say I never dreamed that Shakerism would turn out the way it has. We've been victims of circumstance, I suppose. But we don't need to go into all that."

Sister Jennie shrugged and went briskly on to say that Groveland was abandoned in 1892, when she was fifteen. Most of its members had become too feeble to work. Groveland was the third of the society's communities to go under, and five others soon followed it. As was customary, the Groveland people moved to the nearest surviving Shaker village, which was one that had been established at Watervliet after Mother Ann's death there. It was at Watervliet that Sister Jennie reached twenty-one and elected to enter the order. She

moved to Mount Lebanon in 1930, eight years before
the Watervliet village was given up. "The North Family here needed somebody young and active, she told me,
with a faintly challenging look. "I might as well admit
that I do most of the work here — the marketing, the
meal planning, the cooking, and in the winter I even
tend the furnace. The truth is, I'm about the only one
who can. That's in addition, of course, to making all my
own clothing. Most of the others buy their clothes,
which is contrary to custom, but they are no longer able
to make their own, so it can't be helped. Also, I keep
an eye on things in general, except for finances. What
little money we've accumulated over the years, mostly
from the sale of property but partly from selling the
things we've made, is handled by a more business-
minded member, over at Hancock. I think most of it's
invested — in A.T.&T. and R.C.A. and stocks like that.
If you're wondering how we got our land in the first
place, it came from converts. In the early days, a good
many of the converts were farmers. They gave us whatever land they owned, and if it wasn't conveniently near
one of our villages, we sold it and bought some that was.
That's how Mount Lebanon got started, from a gift.
Our rule is — or perhaps I'd better say was — that a convert must pay all of his worldly debts and settle any
other obligations he may have outside and then make
over to the community he chooses to join whatever
money and property he has left. The agreement — or

Covenant, as we call it — that a convert must sign before he is gathered in is very legal. Signing the Covenant is the final step in becoming a Shaker. An applicant must spend six months with us as a novice first. Nobody has ever been forced to become a Shaker or to remain one. Any one of us is free to return to the world at any time. The only thing is that if you leave after signing the Covenant, you're not allowed to return. And, of course, you can't reclaim your gifts."

The path had brought us down to a broad walk that ran between the dwelling house and the first of the two rows of buildings, and there was another walk between the rows themselves. Just beyond the second row was a meadow in which several cows were grazing. Knee-high grass bordered the walks. The six buildings were at least thirty or forty feet apart, and they all looked even bigger, gaunter, and emptier than they had from the top of the slope. They made me feel uncomfortable. In spite of their size, or perhaps because of it, since it gave them a curiously urban look, they didn't seem quite real in this setting.

Sister Jennie gazed up at the buildings admiringly and sighed. As we strolled along the walk in the direction of the barn, she said, "If this were the old days, we wouldn't even be able to hear ourselves think. These buildings were about the busiest workshops you ever saw then. They were all workshops except that one over there. It used to be the novices' dwelling house and the infirmary. That's where Sister Sarah and Sister Sadie — Sadie Maynard, that is, who is getting a little queer, too — would be living now if we weren't so reduced in our circumstances. Sister Sarah used to be very good at making tape chair seats. Sister Sadie made bonnets. I couldn't begin to tell you how many different trades were carried on in these shops. The North Family did weaving, dyeing, tailoring, hatmaking, shoemaking, broommaking, soapmaking, blacksmithing, metalwork, carpentry, woodworking, seed drying, and goodness knows what else. Practically every family did a lot of different things. And, of course, all the families did a good deal more than just take care of their own needs. The different families in a village used to make things for each other. They all made things to sell to the world, too. We had to carry on some trade with the outside, because we couldn't very well raise everything we needed. We didn't like to do it, though, and we never tried to make more than a fair profit. The North Family's specialties — most of the families had at least one — were brooms and packaged seeds. I'll tell you something that you probably don't know. The Shakers here at Mount Lebanon were the first people in the United States to sell seeds in little packages — you know, the kind you can buy for a dime now in any grocery or hardware store. I mean vegetable seeds, of course. You may have noticed that there aren't any flowers around here.

Shakers have never wasted time on useless things like flowers."

We had reached a gate that opened on the barnyard. At Sister Jennie's suggestion, we turned back toward the dwelling house. "I haven't lived seventy years without learning my own strength," she said cheerfully. As we were passing one of the former shops, a man in overalls suddenly came around the corner of it. He was squat, stoop-shouldered, big-eared, and white-haired, and he was carrying a pail of chicken feed. When he saw us, he stopped, looking startled and uneasy, as if he were not accustomed to encountering strangers. Sister Jennie greeted him with kindly warmth. "This is Brother Curtis White," she said to me. "He keeps me supplied with stovewood, and he's wonderful with chickens. Brother Curtis is sixty years, and he's the youngest member of the family." Then she told Brother Curtis that I was interested in Shakerism. He cleared his throat. "Place was alive forty years ago," he said glumly. "You liked to work here then. I came here as an orphan when I was eleven. Started out sickly, but work made me well. Used to be I'd milk twenty cows and cut a cord of wood every day. I'd cut a cord in three hours — times I've done it in two. Been cutting wood over forty years and I've lost only two toes. Wasn't my fault neither time. Both times, my ax had been ground by somebody else." He nodded to Sister Jennie and then to me. "Ground wrong," he added, and walked away.

Sister Jennie and I continued on to the rear of the dwelling house. A fat, slate-colored cat was sitting on the doorstep of the entrance to the women's side, watching us expectantly. Sister Jennie chuckled. "Old Moses is too polite to scratch or whine when he wants in," she said, opening the door. "He just waits." The cat ducked spryly between my ankles and through the doorway. We followed him into a dim, musty passage, full of sharp turns and lined with closed doors. "We're all very fond of Moses," Sister Jennie said. "He came to us twelve years ago, and we converted him. Shakers aren't supposed to have pets, but cats have always been allowed, because they're useful. They fight mice. Old Moses is going on twenty now. Shakers live forever, even Shaker cats. I suppose you've heard about the longevity of Shakers?" I confessed that I hadn't. "Well, it's a fact," she said. "You almost never hear of a Shaker dying until he's very, very old. We're almost never sick, either. Elder Frederick W. Evans, of this village, who was one of our greatest intellectuals — why, he even corresponded for a while with Tolstoy about cooperative farming and spiritual matters — used to say that no Shaker had any business being sick until he was past sixty. I agree with him. When you lead a pure, disciplined, noncompetitive life, like ours, you just don't have the worries and anxieties that cause illness." She smiled, and added, "People didn't start calling us Shakers because we were all sick and trembly."

"How did the name originate?" I asked.

"Oh, the world's people made it up back in Mother Ann's time, to ridicule the way we worship," she said mildly, halting with her hand on the knob of one of the closed doors and turning to me. "I guess I might as well tell you that our meetings aren't like ordinary church services. They're mostly singing and marching. If you ever saw a Shaker meetinghouse, you'd probably say it looked like a ballroom or a gymnasium. We never had pews or anything like that — just benches around the wall. At the start of our services, there would always be a very short sermon by one of the elders. Then he would call out, 'Go forth and march!,' and the real meeting would begin. Six or eight good singers would form a group in the middle of the room and start a hymn. The rest of us would parade around them, marching two or three abreast. We had to march in step and we had to beat time with our hands in a certain way. Some of the marches were slow, but most of them were fast and lively. We really had to step. We'd keep going for an hour or more, and the faster we marched, the harder we'd be wrestling against the powers of evil. Sometimes, our struggles made us twist and turn. Well, that's what our enemies called shaking. At first, they called us Shaking Quakers, and then just plain Shakers. I don't know how we started using the name ourselves. It wasn't anything to be ashamed of, so I guess we just got into the habit. Besides, Shakerism is a whole lot more than a name." Sister Jennie opened the door abruptly. "We had our last meeting here in Mount Lebanon in 1933, just before we sold the meetinghouse," she said. "We're all too old now to march anyway."

We entered a broad, bare, white-walled foyer, with a steep staircase leading from it to the second floor. Through an open doorway, I caught a glimpse of what was apparently the women's parlor — a large, cheerless room crowded haphazardly with ladder-back chairs. The foyer was furnished only with a long refectory table, above which hung several lurid watercolor views of Venice and Naples, and a rigid but graceful wooden settee, on which three elderly women were sitting, looking like chaperons at a prom. They smiled at us with a kind of sedate excitement. One of them was Sarah Collins. Sister Jennie introduced me to her and to her companions — Eldress Rosetta Stephens and Sister Grace Dahm. Eldress Rosetta, who wore a somber gray Shaker gown, is a tiny, sweet-faced woman of eighty-six. Sister Grace is in her middle seventies, small and round, with short, curly white hair. She was wearing a giddy green-and-lavender house dress. They all had risen upon being introduced, and Sister Sarah, whose dress, though of Shaker cut, was a rich crimson and made of a material that resembled velvet, greeted me with a jovial wink.

"I like a new face," she said.

"We've been watching you through the window,"

Sister Grace said. "We saw you talking to Brother Curtis, and everything."

"Dear Brother Curtis," Eldress Rosetta said. "He never seems to be doing anything, but he's a great help to us. I remember him when he was a little boy. I'm one of the ancients of this city, you know."

"Eldress Rosetta is English," Sister Jennie told me. "She was born in England."

Eldress Rosetta confirmed this modestly. "America is a noble country," she said, "but I grew up in London. My father kept an Aerated Bread shop on the Waterloo Road. Elder Frederick Evans brought me to Mount Lebanon when I was eleven. We met in England, where he was doing missionary work. My father had great respect for the Shakers, and my mother had died, so he let me come with Elder Frederick. We crossed the Atlantic Ocean on the *Great Eastern* in 1872. That was the ship they laid the Atlantic cable with, you know. It was a most magnificent ship. Europe had been combed for costly engravings to decorate it with. It was so grand that none of us children on board were allowed to go about unattended. They were afraid we might damage something, you see. I remember everything about the *Great Eastern* so vividly, more vividly than things that happened only a few years ago. Isn't that strange?"

"Well, I remember Groveland almost better than I do Watervliet," Sister Jennie replied.

"Watervliet was where I lived before I came here,"

Sister Grace said. "I remember it very well. It was nice there, and we had good friends in Albany."

Sister Sarah grinned at me. "I do like a new face," she said.

"We all do," Sister Jennie said gently.

There was a prolonged introspective silence, and then Sister Jennie said that perhaps we had better continue our inspection of the house. "It's almost time for me to start getting supper ready," she explained. "We eat at five-thirty."

We excused ourselves and started for the stairs. "I think I'll just go along with you," Sister Grace said. She got up and joined us, and the two others settled contentedly back on the settee. As we passed the refectory table, I glanced at the water colors above it. "Please don't look at those things," Sister Jennie said. "We're getting more and more lax here, I'm sorry to say. Just because someone gave those pictures to us, we had to put them up. Pictures were never permitted in the old days. Mother Ann always believed that they were distracting, and she knew that they are terrible dust catchers. That's the reason we don't have carpets, either. Tidiness is one of our principal rules. Mother Ann said, 'Clean your room well, for good spirits will not live where there is dirt. There is no dirt in Heaven.' And, look, here's another of our rules." We had reached the stairs, and she placed her right foot on the bottom step. "This is the way we must go upstairs," she said, glancing

sharply at Sister Grace. "Some of us are getting out of
the habit now, but the rule is always the right foot first.
That's for discipline and uniformity. We are also supposed to put our right stocking and shoe on first."

There was no furniture at all in the second-floor hall.
Sister Jennie opened a door at one end of it. "Well, this
is my room," she said. "We each have a room to ourself
now, but the rule used to be two to a room, sometimes
three. First of all, I want you to notice that transom."
The transom, which was open, was a wooden panel fixed
on a vertical center pivot. "Most of our rooms have
them," she said. "They're much more sensible than ordinary transoms, of course, because they create a real
draft. They're something special with Mount Lebanon."
Sister Grace and I followed Sister Jennie inside. It was
a corner room, over twenty feet long and at least fifteen
feet wide, with white plaster walls and two large windows, but it was so full of furniture that it looked small,
cramped, and dark. In it were a narrow, cotlike bed; a
big, square table with drawers; a built-in cabinet with
drawers, which covered most of one wall and rose nearly
to the ceiling; a three-step ladder stool; a chest of drawers; a sewing table; a small, octagonal table; a Morris
chair; a ladder-back rocking chair; and three ladder-back
straight chairs. Two of the straight chairs were hanging
side by side against one wall, suspended from pegs by
the upper slats in their backs. "That's the way Shakers
keep chairs out of the way when they're not in use," Sis-

ter Jennie said. There were no pictures on the walls, but there were two unframed cards with maxims printed on them. One read:

> A man of kindness to his beast is kind.
> Brutal actions show a brutal mind.
> Remember: He who made the brute,
> Who gave thee speech and reason, formed him mute;
> He can't complain, but GOD's omniscient eye
> Beholds thy cruelty. He hears his cry.
> He was destined thy servant and thy drudge,
> But know this: his creator is thy judge.

The other read, "Shun idleness. It is the rust that attaches itself to the most brilliant metals — Voltaire." "Sister Catherine Allen of Mount Lebanon wrote that poem," Sister Jennie said, ignoring Voltaire. "There used to be a copy of it posted in every Shaker barn."

I picked my way around the room, with Sister Jennie sidling along informatively at my elbow and Sister Grace watching us from just inside the door. Except for the Morris chair and the octagonal table, Sister Jennie assured me, all the furnishings were of classic Shaker manufacture. They were made of dark-stained wood and they were as ruthlessly severe and functional as a folding chair, though considerably more handsome. "There isn't a thing in this room that I'd let one of those greedy antique collectors lay a finger on, except over my dead body," Sister Jennie said happily. "Especially that rocker. The Shakers invented the rocking chair, you know, and mine — or, I should say, that one — is probably the oldest in this family. The less said about the Morris chair, the better. I won't deny, though, that it's very comfortable. The octagonal table was made by a neighborhood carpenter and given to us as a gift. We took it in the spirit in which it was given, but it's all wrong. In the first place, it's doodaddy, and in the second place, if you notice, it's made of curly maple. Curly maple is the only wood that the old Shakers never used. They thought it was too ornate."

Sister Grace moved a step or two into the room and gave a timid cough. Sister Jennie looked at her inquiringly. "Would it be all right if I showed him *my* room?" Sister Grace asked eagerly. "I'd like for him to see it, if it's all right." "Why — " Sister Jennie began, but Sister Grace, cutting her short, turned to me and went on in a rush, "There's some very nice furniture in my room, too — and besides I've got a parrot named LeRoy that's over sixty years old and can talk, and a music box that one of the world's people gave me that plays 'A Bicycle Built for Two.' If you could come in for just a minute, I'd give you one of LeRoy's pretty feathers, and you could wear it in your hat."

I glanced at Sister Jennie. Her expression had become a trifle fixed. Then she smiled. "Well, I guess we've seen everything there is to see in here," she said, "so I don't see why not."

Pause for Reflection

The Haft Glass Company, Inc. ("Everything in Glass"), occupies the ground floor of a battered, gray brick, bean-pole loft building on West Forty-second Street, just west of Ninth Avenue. The firm was founded in a basement on Maiden Lane by a Polish immigrant named Nathan Haft in 1857, it moved to its present location in the winter of 1894, and it is one of the oldest glass-and-glazing establishments in New York City. For some years shortly before the First World War, it was also one of the largest and most prosperous, with clients throughout the United States and Canada, but it has long since slumped and shrunken. It is now, though still widely known and highly respected in the trade, little more than a neighborhood store.

I had heard about the Haft Glass Company from one of its occasional customers, and one afternoon when I was over that way, I dropped around for a look at the place. A look was all I got that day. The door, which stands at the end of a twilit vestibule, flanked by a fly-specked display window and a flight of stairs that leads to the floors above, was locked, and just below the knob hung a penciled sign: "Having lunch at Poison Pete's.

Be back. L. Haft." The edges of the card were frayed and
smudged and it was fixed to the panel with a rusty screw.
There was no telling how long it had been there. As I
turned away, I glanced in the display window. It was
dim and dusty and crammed with mirrors, and the first
thing I saw was a staring multitude of myself. Then,
stepping closer, I made out, propped in a corner, another
sign. Like the notice on the door, it was printed in pencil,
on what appeared to be a piece of shirt board. "Whither
goest thou in such haste?" it read. "Pause for reflection.
See yourself as others see you. L. Haft." Nearby, placed
between the mirrors, tilted against the glass, or curling
up from the floor, were others, at least a dozen of them,
similarly signed. I edged along the window, accompanied
by all my faces, and read them. Several were in verse. One
read:

> Count that day lost whose low descending sun
> Sees prices shot to Hell and business done just for fun.

And another:

> What does it matter if he's white or black or blue
> Christian, Mohammed, or Jew.
> Does he have faith in God?
> Then trust him
> He will see you through.

The rest were maxims: "You must stand for something
or fall for anything"; "Some of us learn how to make

money, but how many of us learn how to live"; "You
can't take it with you. Especially if you haven't got it";
"Want to lick cancer? Love they neighbor. That's the
answer. No hatred, no cancer"; and "Don't be sorry if
the bottle is half empty. Be glad it is half full." Partly
obscured by the last was one more. I had to stoop to see
it. It read, "Don't go away mad. Just go away." I straightened up, and did.

A couple of days later, I tried again. This time I had
better luck. It was around three o'clock when I reached
the store and the place looked as deserted as ever, but
the Poison Pete sign was gone and the door was un-
locked. I pushed it open and walked in. Just inside, to
the right, was another door, not quite closed, with a
pinup bathing beauty pasted on the panel. A gritty workbench and an oil-drum trash can stood against the opposite wall. Beyond them stretched a cavern, some ninety
feet deep and twenty feet wide, with a stamped-tin ceiling and a splintered floor. It was creepy with shadows
and smelled of age, and its walls were lined with racks
of sheet glass. In the distance, circling slowly in a furtive
draft, hung a single naked light. The only other light
came from behind the inner door. I went over and gin-
gerly knocked. For a moment, nothing happened. Then,
abruptly, a man's voice said, "You mean it used to be.
But not any more. Pittsburgh Plate is the best in the
world. Has been for thirty years. So forget about France.

How's your brother? . . . Poppycock! . . . Well, give him my regards, and thanks." A telephone clanked in its cradle, a chair scraped, a floor board creaked, and a small, bony, sad-eyed man of indeterminate age appeared at the door. He had on a stiff brown suit and an inconspicuous tie, and he was polishing a pair of rimless glasses with a wisp of Kleenex. "Yes, sir," he said. "What can I do for you?" I introduced myself and told him why I was there. He put on his glasses and stared at me. "My boy," he said, "I hope you haven't come far. Because you're a good many years too late. The Haft Glass Company is practically a thing of the past. However." He stuck out his head. "Glad to meet you. I'm Louis Haft. My grandfather founded this business, my father built it up, and I'm hanging on for dear life. Come on in."

I followed Mr. Haft into a stuffy cubbyhole office. He took my coat and hooked it on a nail on the wall. Then, squeezing past the gaping door of a monstrous, black, four-wheeled iron safe, he sank down at a desk in a corner, tipped back against a pillar of filing cabinets, and yawned. There was an ice-cream-parlor chair at his elbow. I balanced myself on its tiny seat and looked around. The desk was one of three in the room. One of the others filled an entire wall. It was an old-fashioned bookkeeper's desk of the stand-up type, with a waist-high counter, seven feet long and as steep as a roof. A honeycomb of pigeonholes stuffed with old letters and oily rags and sample squares of glass surmounted the counter. Another, somewhat smaller safe sat on the floor underneath. It was surrounded by a litter of empty bottles, and there was a hole in the door where the combination had been. Between the larger safe and a rubbishy heap of corrugated paper boxes stood an ancient roll-top desk, painted black and with brass fittings. On it were a bottle of iodine, a box of Kleenex, a tin of mercurochromed Band-Aids, several jars of highly colored pills, and four framed photographs. Three were conventional studio portraits — a handsome woman, two smiling children, and an elderly couple. The other was a tintype of a bearded old man with a little black *yarmulke* on his head. A small sign, like those in the window, was tacked on the wall above this desk. It read, "Don't wait for the hearse to take you to Church." I glanced at Mr. Haft. He gave a cheerful grunt. "Pretty good, isn't it?" he said. "It hits you with a smile and leaves you with a thought. I wish I could claim it for my own, but I can't. I copied it out of a magazine. My own creations are all in the window out front. I suppose you noticed them?"

I said I had. "Are they all your own creations?" I asked.

"At least half," he said. "The rest, more or less. I may borrow an idea, but I don't often steal. I'll jiggle it around in my head until it comes out my way. So I call them mine. Take the one about pause for reflection. That's a very good example. The words may be old, but the thought is brand-new. Or was twenty years ago. As a matter of fact, that particular sign is the first one I ever made. It's what got me started. The way it happened was pure accident. That was back around 1934. My father was still alive in those days and still running the business, and I was just working for him. So, except when he was off somewhere, I had a certain amount of time to think. Well, I got to thinking one day about our front window. All it had in it was some sample mirrors that had been there since as far back as I can remember. Which is pretty far. I may not look it, but I'll be seventy-two in November. In other words, it was time for a change. It needed some pepping up. I thought of this and I thought of that, and finally I thought of a sign. The minute I did, I had it. It just popped into my mind. I sat right down and wrote it out and stuck in it in the window. I don't know when Pop first noticed it. He never said. Things like that didn't interest him. He never put much stock in advertising. He relied on salesmanship. Otherwise, though, it was a great success. Just the ticket. Everybody stopped and read it. I'd peep out and watch them pull up and look. Then they'd break into a grin. That made me feel pretty cute. It wasn't like the business. It was something I could take full credit for myself. It was mine.

"After that — well, you know how it is. You find something you like to do and you keep on. I guess you might call it my hobby. I enjoy it. It's a way of making friends. You give and you get. I had a big man in the Cancer Society come in just the other day. He was passing by and he read my sign on the subject and it impressed him. He wanted to congratulate me. He thought there might be something in what I said. I think so, too — hatred is the root of every evil — so we had a fine talk. The result was a new friend. I gave and I gained. He wasn't the first. Not by a thousand. It happens all the time. But, of course, Pop was right. From his way of looking at it, I mean. Signs and sayings and philosophy are one thing. Business is another. They don't have much conection. If I had as many customers as I have sign-gazers, I'd be the talk of the town. I'd need an army of people on my pay-roll. As it is, I have three, and only two of them are regular. They do the bulk of the cutting, and they handle all routine deliveries and installations. The other comes in on occasion. According to union regulations, it takes at least three men to move a sheet of glass of over a hundred and fifty united inches. United means length plus width. I'm everything else — office, estimator, and sales force. Pop had close to a dozen men at his peak. That was in addition to me and the rest of the family. I have two younger brothers and four sisters. When necessary, we all pitched in. There were times when Pop could have used almost any number. For quite a while, he did well over a hundred thousand dollars' worth of business every year. That was back when a dollar meant something, too. The best I can do is a fraction of that. I could tell you exactly, but who cares? Except me. My brother Mark was the first to pull out. Then, one by one, the girls got married and scattered. Abe stayed on till 1934. He's in business for himself now, and doing well. So is Mark, I hear. He's in ladies' sportswear. I'm not surprised at how they've done. They're a lot like Pop, in some ways. They're hustlers. My trouble is I'm not. Naturally, I like to make a profit. I'm not sitting here all day for my health. But I don't have much interest in burning up the world. Never did. I just take what comes my way. When the Lord made me, He left something out. I don't agree that time is money. I think money is time.

"In that respect, I take after my grandfather. That's him on the desk over there — the old fellow with the beard. The others are Pop and my mother, my wife, and my two grandchildren. Jeffrey's sixteen and little Randy is ten. They're my daughter Helene's children. Her husband is a professional man. He's a lawyer. Those four — Helene and her family — are about all I've got left of anything. I have dinner with them at their place up on West Seventy-ninth Street every Wednesday and Friday night. The rest of the time, I'm here. It's the nearest thing I've got to a home. I live in the West Eighties, but as far as I'm concerned, that's only a place to sleep. There's nothing else there any more. Mama and Pop both died in 1941. Then, six years ago, I lost my wife. A wonderful, wonderful woman. She — But we won't go into that. And, of course, Grandpa has been dead for years. Since 1894, to be exact. I remember him, though. He was just the kind of man he looks. Everybody loved him. Good and kind and knew his trade to perfection, but no push. The drive was missing. No matter how hard he worked, nothing seemed to happen. His heart just wasn't in business. All he asked was to make a living. Live and let live. His family and the synagogue, they were his life. Especially the synagogue. He was a member of Congregation Shaare Zedek, down on Henry Street, for almost forty years. Most of that time, he was its president.

"So was Pop, as a matter of fact. He was elected in 1924. Not down on Henry Street, of course. Shaare Zedek moved up to West Ninety-third Street, where it is now, sometime before that. But it was odd, wasn't it? The coincidence, I mean. There wasn't anything odd about picking Pop for president. He was the right man in every way. I doubt if they ever had a better. He had ability, and he had devotion. He was truly religious. The Sabbath meant something to him. Pop had three big pleasures in life. He loved pinochle, he loved a nice whiskey toddy, and he dearly loved a good cigar. The kind he liked was called Madison Avenue. They were handmade and three for a dollar, and he never smoked less than fifteen a day. Except Saturday. He remembered the Sabbath. Nothing interfered. He kept it holy."

Mr. Haft was silent for a moment. Then he took out his watch, gave it a glance, and carefully put it away. His chair dropped back to the floor. "I like a good cigar myself," he remarked. "Also, about this time of day, I generally take a little refreshment. Will you join me in a drink? Or maybe you'd rather have something else." He swung around to the row of filing cabinets and pulled open one of the drawers. "Let's see," he said, peering in. "The cupboard's kind of bare today. Peppermints? Salted peanuts? Gumdrops? Or can I offer you a Hershey bar or a Milky Way? I'm afraid that's about all there is."

"A drink would be fine," I said. "I don't often eat candy."

"No?" Mr. Haft said. "Well, neither do I. I don't dare. I only keep it for the sake of hospitality. Some people don't drink. But then somebody drops in — a customer or a salesman or whatever — I like to be able to offer them something. I'm funny. I prefer a smile to a frown. So I do what I can to get it. And then, of course, there's the kids in the neighborhood. When they get hungry for candy, they all know where to come. For me, though, the stuff is poison. One bite, and I'd be as sick as a cat for a week." He slammed the drawer and opened another. There was a clink of glass on glass. He took out a bottle of bourbon about two-thirds full and two whiskey glasses and stood them on his desk. Then he reached back in the drawer and brought up a handful of bread sticks wrapped in a paper napkin. He shook a drift of bread crumbs from one of the glasses, filled it to the brim with whiskey, and handed it to me. "To tell the truth," he said, filling the other glass, "there isn't much I can eat. The doctors have me on a very strict diet. I live on dry meat, boiled potatoes, hard rolls, and bananas. My stomach started acting up in the summer of 1926 and it's never been the same since. The reason I remember so well is Pop went to Europe that year and left me here in full command. That was some year. It would have been bad enough even if I'd felt like myself. We still had some business then. Quite a bit. So much so that all the time Pop was gone — twelve months — I took exactly four days off. Including Saturdays and Sundays. And most of the time I was so sick I could hardly lift the phone. It was torture." Mr. Haft shook his head and raised his glass. "Fortunately," he said, "whiskey doesn't seem to bother me. If I eat a little something along the way, it even seems to help. Well, here's to you and me and the brotherhood of man."

We swallowed our drinks. Mr. Haft shuddered, put down his glass, and broke off an end of bread stick. He popped it into his mouth and nodded toward the bottle. "How about another?" he suggested.

"Not right now," I said.

Mr. Haft looked relieved. "Good," he said. "I agree. We'll enjoy it more later. After we've had a look at the shop. Such as it is. But first, a good drink calls for a good cigar." He turned again to the filing cabinets. "I get these up the street," he said, sliding a box of pale panatelas across the desk. "In my opinion, they're the best there is. They're no Madison Avenue, of course. That's been out of the picture for years. But they're clear Havana and they're made right. And don't be bashful. Nobody else is. Take a couple. You'll want one for after dinner."

When we had lighted our cigars, Mr. Haft cleared away the bottle and the glasses and returned the box to its drawer. The bread sticks he left on the desk. He then leaned comfortably back in his chair and blew a long plume of smoke at the ceiling. "My first today," he said. "The doctor recommends I hold off until my lunch has had time to settle. Otherwise, there's apt to be trouble. Pop usually had his first cigar going before he was half through breakfast. Well, I'm not the man he was. By no stretch of the imagination. Least of all when it comes to health. Pop was made of iron. To the best of my knowledge, he was never what you'd call sick but one day in his life. That was the day he died. I remember he called me into his room that evening. He was sitting there, with a cigar in his mouth and a glass of whiskey at his side, holding his left wrist. 'Louie,' he told me, 'I've got an evil pain. Nothing seems to help. I think I'm going.' I tried to tell him different — it didn't seem possible — but he knew. He passed away in the night. He went to sleep and never woke up. It was his heart. He'd gone full speed for eighty-one years and it finally just gave out. Pop had every natural gift. He was a born businessman. He had fight and he had brains and he had quick decision. But that wasn't all that took him to the top. The main reason was he was bound and determined to get there. I told you my grandfather founded this firm. He did. In the year 1857, he rented a room in a basement down on Maiden Lane and he hung out his sign. That was how we began. So he started it. But it was Pop that made it a business. In a way, he came up fast. Take this building, for example. We own it. Five of us — my four sisters and me — we all hold equal shares. It's been in the family since 1894. Pop built it when he was only thirty-four. On the other hand, he started early. He was an only child and he had to do his share. Grandpa had him cutting glass before he was hardly ten, and at fifteen he was already out getting orders. In 1879, when he and Mama got married, he was practically in charge. He was still a long way from seeing daylight, though. Pop never talked much about those early years, but he did tell me one time the story of their wedding day. They got married in a hall down on Fourteenth Street. After the knot was tied, they came out and started for home. When they reached the corner where the horsecars for Henry Street stopped, Pop opened his purse and took out a nickel and handed it to Mama. 'What's this for?' she wanted to know. Her carfare, he told her. 'My carfare,' she said. 'What about you, Isaac?' Pop said he hemmed and hawed and tried to change the subject, but he finally had to tell the truth. He was going to walk. That one nickel was all the money he had. 'In that case,' Mama said, 'we'd better save it. We'll both walk.'

"That also shows you the kind of mother I had. Pop

married a real partner. She even learned how to cut glass. Not just for fun, either. She was willing to work at it. I've seen her tackle a job that would daunt the average man, and come through with flying colors. And she had a head on her. She and Pop only lived on Henry Street for about a year before they moved uptown. The reason they moved was Mama. There wasn't any future on the lower East Side, she decided, and the best way to get established uptown was to live there. The first place they lived was a flat at Eighth Avenue and Forty-second Street, and that's where I was born and got my start. After that, we lived all over this part of town — four or five different flats and rooming houses — but I don't have much memory of any of them. Except for a few little glimpses, all my earliest recollections are centered right here. This building is more than just the place where the Haft Glass Company really began. For a good many years, it was home. Pop built it with that in mind. The basement and the fourth and fifth floors were for storage, the third floor was our workroom, we had our office and more storage space on the ground floor and the second floor was a great big apartment that ran right through the building. It was my impression the day we moved in that Pop had made us a palace. Compared to what we'd known before, it was. The windows were always full of sun and we got any breeze that was stirring. It was the last word. We had the first telephone for blocks around. It hung on the side wall there, a little beyond that long crack. I remember the people trooping in just for the novelty of looking at it. And we had the first electric lights. We were the first in that department for what seemed like years. Pop did it by special arrangement with the trolley company. When they started work on the Forty-second Street line, he went right down and had a talk with one of the engineers. The result was, as soon as their power lines reached this block, they made a tap and ran a wire in to us. I don't know how much it cost. Probably plenty. But that was the way Pop operated. He had vision. Better light meant better work.

"I remember the difference. I'd been down in the shop for quite a few years when the lights came on. I started full time at the age of thirteen. I didn't exactly have to. It wasn't the way it had been with Pop. The days of struggle were over. But I'd taken all the schooling I cared for — I had seven years at P.S. 67 — and he could use me. Not that he ever said so. He didn't need to. It was understood. The business was beginning to soar and every little bit helped. In Grandpa's day, we were about what we are now. We distributed glass and installed it. Glass and mirrors. Pop broadened out and became a jobber as well. That's when the volume zoomed. Our specialty was tenement houses. Pop knew all the contractors — they were his friends. He liked them all and they all liked him. When their business boomed, we boomed along with it. It's hard to believe it now, but back in those days if we didn't supply and glaze the sash in at least four hundred tenement houses, we thought we'd had a bad year. That was our bread and butter. Our cake was stores and clubs and fine Fifth Avenue mansions. Pop had contacts all over the country. One of the biggest was an English concern that operated in Canada. Every year, around Christmas, a cab would pull up out front and half a dozen Englishmen would come marching in. That was the signal to break out the cigars and start the whiskey flowing. Maybe they'd come back two or three days in a row. At the end, they'd settle up for the work we had done that year and Pop would sign a contract for the next. I say 'sign.' That's only a manner of speaking. Pop never signed a contract in his life. He didn't consider it necessary. His word was as good as his bond, and he assumed the same of everybody else. If they failed him, that was the last of them. I've seen him lend a business acquaintance as high as five thousand dollars, and nothing passed between them but the money and a handshake. On some of the big jobs we did, price wasn't even discussed. They knew that when the bill arrived, it wouldn't be a penny more than right. Who can do that now? Pop was old-fashioned. He was an honest man.

"I don't mean that honesty was the secret of Pop's success. If it was, we'd still be right up at the top. I feel as strongly on that subject as he ever did. When I hear a lie, my whole inside reacts. The secret of Pop's success was Pop. And the times. We began to slip in the depression. Then I took over. That was too much for it. You could hardy expect a business to recover from two straight blows like that. I've managed to hold on to most of our old customers. They still call up. But I doubt very much if I'm still getting all of their business. They don't have the same old fire in their voice. I don't suppose I'll ever completely lose them. Or fail to pick up a new one every now and then. The name of Haft still means something. It's been an honorable name for three generations, and I think I can say that I haven't spoiled it yet. The only thing wrong with this business is me. I'm just not shrewd enough. I'll give you an example. I had a steady customer some years ago. He came in every couple of weeks, always bought a few dollars' worth of glass — and always paid cash. That's the way it went until one day he was a quarter short. He said he'd pay me later. Pop was still alive then, and I don't remember how it came about, but that night I happened to mention it to him. 'Louie,' he said, 'you've made a mistake. Never let that type of man owe you anything. What you should have said was forget it. Then he'd come back. Now he won't. You'll never see that man again. He'll go to somebody else.' Well, Pop was right. That was the end of my steady customer. Pop was really a wonder. He was my teacher for sixty years, but I never quite caught up with him. It's a little like a fellow that used to work here back in the twenties. He dropped in one day a couple of years ago, just to say hello, and we got to talking about cutting glass and one thing led to another until finally he challenged me to a contest. I've forgotten what it involved — who could cut the best freehand oval, or some such. Anyway, when I won, he was amazed. 'I don't understand it,' he told me. "Why, it was you that taught me how to cut glass. You told me all I know.' 'Sure,' I said. 'But I didn't tell you everything I know.' That's the way it was with me and Pop. Everything I learned about business, I learned from him. Only, he didn't tell me everything *he* knew. I guess he figured it wouldn't make much difference."

The telephone gave a sudden stuttering peal. Mr. Haft turned and stared. "Probably the wrong number," he said. "It usually is. However . . ." He plucked the receiver to his ear. "Haft speaking. Oh, hello, Dave." There was a pause. "Well, that didn't take you long. Nice work." He shook his head. "No. No, I guess not. . . . O.K." Mr. Haft hung up, took a last pull at his cigar, and stubbed it out in an ashtray. "That was one of my men," he told me. "They've just finished up a little job down at London Terrace and they're coming right in. Consequently, if I'm going to show you around the shop, maybe we'd better get started. We don't want them breathing down our neck."

I said I was ready. Mr. Haft stretched and pushed back his chair. I edged after him, around the open safe and through the door and out into the dim immensity of the shop. After the office, it looked bigger and darker than ever. We headed down a rumbling aisle toward the lonely light at the rear. Mr. Haft waved a pallid hand. "Most of these racks are general stock," he said. "Window lights and picture glass of various grades and thickness — across-the-counter stuff — and what they call opal glass. Opal is flashed on one surface. There's a coating to diffuse the light. Photo-engravers use it, and X-ray people. I've also got a certain amount of colonial glass. Colonial-type, I should say. It's fake. A factory in England makes it for the antique trade. I'm one of the few I know that will bother with it. Every now and then, though, I get a call from some lady decorator. The bulk of the big stuff — heavy plate and mural mirrors and partition-size frosted and wire and corrugated glass — is down in the basement or up on the third floor. All the other floors, including our old flat, are let for lofts. We don't need them. Or, rather, the way things are now, there's more profit in rent. At least, it's regular."

We skirted a final barricade of racks and emerged into a dingy clearing flooded with dingy light. There were shelves stacked with cans of paint and putty and linseed oil along the two side walls. The rear wall was a row of gray, faintly daylit windows. Below one of the windows was a rickety grindstone. In the middle of the clearing, directly beneath the dangling bulb, sat a huge worktable, surrounded by a sleet of broken glass. It was rooted to the floor on eight great legs and its surface was covered with a padding of faded gold-and-crimson carpet. On it lay a brass-tipped wooden square, a couple of brass-tipped rules, and a cigar box full of ten-cent-store glass cutters. Mr. Haft picked up one of the cutters and felt the cutting wheel. "Dry as a bone," he said. He walked over to the nearest shelf, rummaged around for a moment, and came back with a two-foot scrap of window glass and a saucer of what smelled like kerosene. He dropped the pane on the table in front of him and set the saucer nearby. Then he fixed me with a happy smile. "Now, my boy," he said, "I'm going to give you a little demonstration. I imagine you've seen glass cut before. Probably many a time. But I very much doubt if you've ever seen the job done right. Anybody can learn to handle a cutter. I could teach you enough in a couple of hours to get you into the union. But teaching and experience will carry you just so far. If you're going to cut glass so it means something, you've got to have the gift. Style can't be bought. You're either born with the feeling or you're not. I've got my limitations, but not when it comes to glass. I understand it. I've got that seventh sense. Even Pop admitted that."

Mr. Haft cleared his throat. "We'll begin with the cutter," he said, holding it up. "There are two important things. First, how to hold it. Only one way is right — between the first and second fingers, with the thumb coming in against the side to steady it. Like so. It's the way some people hold a pencil. Except, notice the angle.

The shaft stands almost perpendicular. I'd call it ninety degrees. The second thing is the cutter itself. Before I can cut, the cutting wheel must be lubricated. We don't use diamond-point cutters any more. For most work, hard steel is better. Also, a diamond-point cutter is a one-man tool. The owner shapes it to his way. If you use my diamond cutter, you'll ruin it for me. So steel is more convenient. Ideas on lubrication differ. Some prefer turpentine. But to me there is nothing but kerosene. The other is too hard. Kerosene has a softness, a gentleness. It's just right. Watch how I dip it in — just the cutting wheel, and just long enough. Now we're ready to start. The object is a straight break from top to bottom, cut freehand but true. So you can see what happens, I'll go slow. Once the wheel is in position, nothing moves but my arm. Not the fingers. The arm muscles make the sweep. But the pressure comes from the fingers. And the pressure is firm. Listen for the whine — the squeal. Hear it? That means I'm cutting glass. If there's no whine, you're only scratching. But look — perfection! Every inch an even bite. And, of course, as straight as a rule. The secret was the pressure. I wasn't afraid to give it some muscle. Fear is why so many cutters never really learn. You can't count on them. The average cutter is like everybody else. He's afraid of glass. He doesn't understand it. Down deep, it's got him buffaloed. This is classed as a dangerous trade. His mind is always worrying about accidents — bloody wounds. He may not think it is, but his muscles know better. The result is every so often they react against him. Then comes too light a cut, and a ruined piece of glass. You can't go over a cut a second time. It won't break evenly. It won't even start. That's the next step — to start the break. A little tap with the back of the cutter on the underside will do it. Once, twice, and done. See the little spot of cloud? Now the glass is weak from top to bottom along the cut and ready to break. They way to break it depends on the size. If this were a big piece, I'd slide a rule underneath, on a line with the cut, and press on the tilted side. But for one this small, and because I know how, my hands are enough." Mr. Haft put the cutter aside. Then he gripped the pane with both hands, one on each side of the cut, near where the cloud had appeared. "Notice that the cut surface is up," he said. "And how when I snap, the pressure is down. Away from the cut. Always down and away from the cut, and always — like this — quick!" He snapped. There was a sudden crack and an echoing tinkle. He held out two cleanly parted panes.

"Very nice," I said.

"Fair," Mr. Haft said. "I see a couple of chips. Probably a flaw in the glass. But no matter." He discarded the smaller of the panes and slid the other over in front of me. "Now, then," he said, retrieving the cutter. "Let's see how much you've learned. Here — take a sweep. Just for the fun of it."

I took the cutter from him and slipped it between my

fingers, and brought the cutting wheel down on the glass.

"A little more angle," Mr. Haft said. "Just a — that's it. O.K. Let her rip." I pressed, and drew the cutter carefully back. But it didn't rip. It was like trying to cut ice with a stick. The wheel skittered across the pane, leaving behind a faint and wavering scratch. I looked at Mr. Haft.

"Not bad," he said. "I've seen some beginners do worse. You could learn. But it's a little harder than it looks, isn't it?"

"Quite a bit," I said. "I suppose heavy glass is even harder."

"Harder?" Mr. Haft said. "You mean to cut? No. Just the opposite. Window glass is far more difficult. That's why I used it to show you. Look at the thickness of that piece. It's barely three thirty-seconds of an inch. The only kind that takes more skill is picture glass. That runs to one-sixteenth or less. What makes glass hard to cut isn't strength. It's weakness. You have to put some pressure behind the cutter with any type of glass. But when you're working on thin glass, you have to gauge it just right. Go too easy and you ruin it. Go too hard and it shatters. When you get into heavy glass, the only problem is making a good clean cut. It all cuts. Except, of course, glass brick. Even wire glass. If you break it right, a bend or two will snap the wire. As a general thing, the better the glass, the easier it is to work. The easiest glass I ever cut was the best they ever made. It was Belgian plate from a special factory in the town of Charleroi. American glass is hard to beat these days, but nobody makes that kind of plate any more. It was a treat to touch it. It cut like butter."

Mr. Haft reached out and picked up the cutter. He ran the wheel slowly across his thumb. "As a matter of fact," he said, "I've still got some — a few odds and ends. I guess they go back to Maiden Lane. I ought to get rid of it, I suppose. I know Pop would. It's junk and takes up space. But I like to go up every once in a while and sort of take a look at it. In a way, it . . . I don't know." He shrugged. "I guess we all do a lot of things." Mr. Haft turned and pitched the cutter into the cigar box. "Well, suppose we go back to the office," he said. "My feeling is that it's time for that other drink."

Shore Whaler

SHORE whaling, the pursuit and capture of whales by a small company of oarsmen in a boat launched from the beach, is a harsh and perilous form of fishery that was evolved by the Puritan settlers of southeastern Long Island in the middle of the seventeenth century and carried on there by their descendants, with an almost ritualistic ferocity, until around 1910. By then, the North Atlantic right whale, to which they were partial, had nearly vanished from the North Atlantic. Shore whaling had ceased some years before that to be very profitable. A generation has now passed since the last chase, and there will probably never be another, but about a dozen Long Island whalemen are still alive. They are all in their seventies or eighties, they are all more or less cousins, they all reside in either East Hampton or Amagansett, and they are the only surviving shore whalers in the world. One of the spryest and unquestionably the most experienced of them is a calm, soft-spoken patriarch named Everett Joshua Edwards, who lives in East Hampton. During his shore-whaling career, he participated in fifteen successful hunts, including one in February, 1907, that resulted in the capture of the fifty-four-foot right whale whose skeleton dominates the Hall of Ocean Life at the American Museum of Natural History; and it was he who killed the last right whale ever taken on the Eastern seaboard. That was six miles off the Amagansett beach, in the summer of 1918.

Most of the few remaining shore whalers have been in retirement for years. Edwards is still gainfully active. He could have dropped comfortably into a rocking chair long ago, but he despises idleness. "I enjoy laying hold," he says. His principal hold is on the presidency and managership of the Home Water Company, in East Hampton, which supplies the village with drinking water, and he also has a good grip on much of its stock. He has headed the company since 1931, succeeding his father-in-law, the late Jeremiah Huntting, who was one of its organizers. Edwards' duties at the water company take up most of his time, but he has other rewarding interests. He is secretary-treasurer of Edwards Brothers & Co., a fraternal partnership that operates a fish dock, three gasoline draggers, and a ship chandlery at Promised Land, a snug cove some five miles northeast of East Hampton, on Gardiners Bay. The business was established by Edwards and two of his three brothers, Herbert and Samuel, in 1916. Samuel, who lives in Amagansett, is president of the firm. Herbert, the eldest of the brothers and Everett's senior by two years, died in 1941. The fourth brother, David, is an East Hampton physician. Edwards also has money in the H. W. Sweet Shipyard & Machine Works, in Greenport, and he is a director of the Osborne Trust Company, the East Hampton bank. His activities have always been numerous. From 1904 to 1908 and from 1910 to 1918, he was clerk of the Town of East Hampton, which includes East Hampton, Amagansett, Montauk, and part of Sag Harbor. For a couple of years in the late nineties, he ran a grocery store in Amagansett, and between 1901 and 1917 he was the proprietor of a drugstore in East Hampton.

Despite this abundance of circumstantial evidence, Edwards does not consider himself a businessman and never has. In some humors, it riles him to be taken for one. He explains that he drifted into business by accident and was swept helplessly and unwillingly away. "I've got a head for figures, and I'm not mortally afraid of the work," he say, "but I'm not a real businessman. For one thing, I lack the constitution. I'm bothered by desk pains." Edwards prefers to think of himself as, and in fact he is, a retired fisherman. "I've fished for the table since," he says, "but I really come ashore in 1930. The fishing turned poor. Up to then, no matter what, I was generally on the water. I pulled seine in the surf, I handlined for cod, and I set ocean traps. When there was whaling, I whaled. I had my master's-and-pilot's license at twenty-one, and from beginning to end I went bunkering in season." Bunkers, or menhaden, are a species of inedible fish, being intolerably bony and oily, but they are commercially useful in the manufacture of fertilizer and medicinal oils. They are caught with capacious drawstring nets known as purse seines. In the course of Edwards's nearly fifty years on the water, he was captain of a succession of bunker-fishingboats — among them a hundred-and-seventy-six-foot steamer, the *Amagansett* — that worked out of Promised Land. One June day in 1910, the *Amagansett*, with Edwards and a crew of thirteen aboard, wallowed into port with a load of nearly two million bunkers — the largest haul ever made by a Long Island bunker boat. "We were mainly awash all the way from Boston Bay," he says, "but I was young and greedy then, and bunkering paid. The fact of the matter is the only clear money I ever made came out of the ocean. 'Twas all fish money, one way or another."

Edwards is seventy-eight years old. He stands six feet one in his stocking feet and weighs close to two hundred pounds. He is big-boned and broad-shouldered, his step is firm, and, unlike many tall men, he holds his head high. His gaze is serene but a trifle intimidating. He has a hard jaw, a straight and thin-lipped mouth, and prominent cheekbones, and his eyes are cold and gray and shadowed by an unruly lock of glacially white hair that falls across his forehead. He has been formally designated a handsome man. This unusual distinction was conferred upon him by Arnold Genthe, the photographer. It was recorded in the February 1, 1937, issue of

Vogue, in an article entitled "The Handsomest Man I Have Ever Photographed," to which Genthe and each of several other notable cameramen contributed a study in male beauty. Genthe encountered Edwards during a week-end visit to East Hampton in the summer of 1933 and within an hour of their meeting had wheedled him into sitting for a portrait. Genthe was so persuasive that he even induced Edwards to change from a business suit to a set of greasy oilskins. "I didn't much care for having my picture taken in my old work clothes," Edwards says, "but I obliged him." His expression in the portrait is stern and somewhat dazed. This look was interpreted by Genthe and the editors of *Vogue* as evincing a "fearlessness and pride of race [that] can give the classical mold cards and spades." The classical mold was adequately represented by the other nominees, who included Ronald Colman, Gary Cooper, Jack Whiting, and the Duke of Kent. Edwards was not annoyed by Genthe's tribute, but he is disinclined to dwell upon the incident. "It surprised me a little," he says. "Yes, it did. The others were all young fellows. Mr. Genthe must have looked at me cross-eyed."

Neither Edwards's good looks nor the state of his health has been noticeably impaired by time. His appearance has not altered since the day it first excited Genthe's admiration, and he says he still feels as nimble as ever. He is, however, a diabetic. He has been afflicted with this ailment for five years, but he insists that it rarely inconveniences him. "It's like the desk pains," he says. "When the desk pains come on, I stand up for a spell. I ward off the diabetes by standing up when there's pie or pudding put on the table. That way, and with insulin. I leave my diabetes mostly to my wife and my brother Dr. Dave." Edwards's confidence in his continuing physical powers is not misplaced. Just before his seventy-seventh birthday, he almost succeeded in tipping and emptying a sixteen-foot dory, beached in his daughter's backyard, that was three-quarters full of rain water. He had wrestled with the boat for an hour and was beginning to ease it over when a couple of neighbors came along and, ignoring his protests, gave him a hand. "I guess we hurt the old man's pride," one of them said later, "but there was a ton of water in that boat. He might have busted himself wide open." A few months later Edwards snatched a spade from a trench digger for his water company who, he decided, was idling, and finished the job himself. He attributes his undiminished strength to the will of God, an unusually happy marriage, and five lifelong precautions. "I don't toy with my food," he explains, "I won't carouse, I've never drunk rum except to keep out the cold, I go to bed when night comes, and I keep my head covered outdoors." On Sunday, when Edwards and his wife, Florence, emerge from their house only for church (like most deeply rooted eastern Long Islanders, they are Presbyterians), he covers his head with a sedate fedora. Every other day of the year, he wears a black, high-

crowned, turn-of-the-century pilot's cap. Caps of this
sort are no longer on the market; his are made for him
by a marine-outfitting firm near Fulton Fish Market. His
dress is otherwise conventionally inconspicuous. He fa-
vors gray suits, blue shirts with unconstricting collars,
and sensible, hump-toed tan shoes. A thick gold chain
hangs across his vest, anchored at one end by a heavy
gold watch and at the other by a heavier, bone-handled
jackknife. He wears a Masonic emblem in his button-
hole.

Mrs. Edwards, a small, bustling, bright-eyed woman of
seventy-four, shares her husband's conviction that their
marriage has been an extraordinarily happy one. She
was seventeen when they were married, in 1892. Edwards
was twenty-one and had seven hundred and forty-three
dollars, all clear fish money, in the Sag Harbor Savings
Bank. "I don't recall that we ever had but one little
difference," Mrs. Edwards said the other day, "and that
was long ago. What happened was Everett grew a mustache. It came in red, and it was big and prickly. Oh, I
didn't care for it at all. We had words about that mustache off and on for weeks, until one night I ended it. I
waited until Everett fell asleep and then I got up and
fetched a pair of scissors and snipped it off. I saved his
good looks. With that awful mustache, I'm sure Everett
would never have got his picture in *Vogue*." Edwards
often feels that he owes his wife an even greater debt of
gratitude. He likes to claim that it is possible that by

marrying him she saved his life. "Around the time we met," he says, "I was aiming to try and ship on a deep-sea whaler. There were still a few old whalers putting out. Miss Florence Huntting changed my mind. I had too much sense to turn my back on a pretty girl like that for forty-four months. If it hadn't been for her, though, I'd have gone. Then, the chances are, I'd have been lost among the icebergs, like my mother's Uncle Rance Conkling. Last seen, he was on a bull whale's back, heading for the South Pole."

Edwards and his wife make their home in a substantial two-story faded brown shingle house on David's Lane. He built the place shortly before his retirement from the sea. It is neither the smallest nor the largest house on the block, but it is somewhat less humble than the cottages inhabited by most retired fishermen. They live comfortably but modestly. Edwards drives to and from his several offices in a creaky old Dodge coupé, and his wife has always done all her own housework. They have two children, both married — Clifford Conkling Edwards and Mrs. Arnold E. Rattray — who reside in East Hampton, and six grandchildren and one great-grand-child, and there are nieces and nephews of various genera-tions. Mrs. Rattray is the wife of the editor-and-publisher of the East Hampton weekly *Star*, and she reports and writes much of the news in the paper. She also found time, some years ago, to write, in collaboration with her father, a history of American shore whaling, entitled "Whale Off!," which was published by Stokes in 1932 and favorably received. Clifford Edwards is a lawyer. With the exception of Dr. Edwards, he is the first male Edwards in eleven generations who hasn't fished, clammed, or whaled for a living. "Clifford is a fine boy and a fine lawyer," his father has said, "but I'd just as soon he hadn't stayed ashore. He surprised me. The Edwardses have always been as fishy as could be."

Edwards has lived in East Hampton the better part of his life, but he is not a native of the village. He was born in Amagansett, which his ancestors helped settle in the sixteen-eighties, on August 10, 1871, and he grew up there. "I rarely set foot here in town till I was full-grown," he says. "Never much cared to. Us 'Gansett boys liked it where we were." Amagansett is three miles east of East Hampton and a hundred and ten miles east of New York. Except for the straggling hamlet of Montauk, which emerged from the wilderness just before the First World War, it is the most easterly village in the state. It is situated on the scrawny neck of the Montauk Peninsula. It overlooks the ocean, half a mile to the south, across a wind-swept expanse of dunes and beach. There is a desolation of moorland just to the east. To the west and north are potato fields and a low wooded ridge that shelters it only slightly from Gardiners Bay. In spite of its exposed position, it is a snug and peaceful place. Its wandering main street is a hundred and fifty feet wide and lined with picket fences, weathered elms and maples, and comfortable, stooped old houses in deep and shadowy lawns. Several of these houses were built in the seventeenth century. Its population is about a thousand. East Hampton is a little larger than Amagansett, a little older, and a little less withdrawn, but the two are much alike and they have always been closely linked. Both are traditionally oriented toward New England rather than New York, both remained almost motionless throughout the eighteenth and nineteenth centuries, and both within the last generation have more than doubled in size.

The spirited growth of East Hampton and Amagansett vexes Edwards. He cannot reconcile himself to it. In his opinion, they have become unwieldy. He is even more rigidly persuaded that their growth has been accompanied by an abysmal decline in manners, morals, and economic stability. " 'Up-to-date' don't mean a thing to me," he says. "I'm old-fashioned. I believe in long drawers and keeping the Sabbath and the best good for all hands. I've see a lot of changes around here, but I can't say I've noticed much improvement. There's more rich and there's more poor. There's less working and there's more worrying. If I was a few years younger, I might feel some different. I wouldn't remember so well how things used to be out here on the East End. I was twenty-four years of age before the railroad arrived. All the time I was growing up, Sag Harbor was the end of the line. That was an hour or more away by stage. We were out of touch and glad of it, especially us 'Gansetters. Nobody ever had it better than we did. We lived off the land and the sea. There were few drunkards and no road-houses, and plenty to eat and a good bed to sleep in for all. Everybody was fishy. Wasn't a boy I knew wouldn't rather be a whaleman than the President of the United States. Then the summer people come. There had been a few before, off and on, and mostly in East Hampton, but 'twasn't till 1895, when we got the railroad, that anybody paid much attention to them. Ever since, it's been mortgage the farm and easy money and fall in step with the boarders. In the old days, New York City was Fulton Fish Market. Now it's Wall Street. I don't put the blame here or there. Good or bad, it can't be helped. But, by the gods, I'd like to see things back the way they were when I was a boy. Yes, I would."

Edwards is haunted happily by the past. Reminiscence rejuvenates him. His voice quickens when he speaks of his youth, and his face softens and his eyes warm and widen. All his early years are wonderfully vivid to him, but it is of whaling and his father, Joshua Edwards, that he most often talks. They dominate his memory and they are inseparable in his mind. "Pop was a whaleman," he says. "I guess he was about the best they ever had around here. The reason us 'Gansetters whaled harder and

longer than anybody else was mainly my father. He led
all the chases. There were close to fifty whales taken off
this stretch of beach in his time, and he killed all but
one. It wasn't just the money. A fifty-footer — what we
called a big one — would bring better than two thousand
dollars in bone and oil back then, but it was more than
that to him. He loved whaling. Never got enough. Always wild to go. I remember once, when I was little, ask-
ing him wasn't he afraid of a whale. 'Yes, yes,' he said.
'I generally try to keep clear of him.' Pop was really rank.
He was eighty-five years of age when he died, in 1915,
and he went off the beach almost to the end. He saw it
all. The first part of his life, he was a deep-sea whaler,
around the Horn and up in the arctic. I remember him
telling how they were chased through the Bering Strait,
during the Civil War, by the Rebel privateer the *Shenan-
doah*. He started in at twenty, as soon as a chance made,
as a harpooner on the *Ontario*, out of Sag Harbor. Nobody had to show him how. He was a 'Gansett boy, so he
knew. Altogether, he made five deep-sea voyages, ending
up on the *Jireh Perry*, out of New Bedford, as first mate.
When he come home for good, in 1868, deep-sea whaling
was mostly over. He and Mother got married that year,
and they built a house on a twenty-five-acre farm he had
from his father. It was just off Main Street, on Whip-
poorwill Lane, and that's where I was born and raised.
It's still there, but we had to let it go after Mother died,

in 1929. City people own it now. There isn't any Whip-
poorwill Lane any more. They call it Atlantic Avenue.
Even our old house has got a name to it — I forget what.
I generally look the other way when I go by.

"Pop didn't farm much. I guess he was too fishy. He
whaled when he could, and when he couldn't whale, he
fished. At one time, he went after sturgeon. Used to be
plenty of them right off the coast here. He was in the
Russian-caviar trade. What they did was ship the roe to
New York, and there was somebody there who shipped
it to Russia, and the Russians put their fancy labels on
it and shipped it back to New York. There was many an
American millionaire ate Long Island caviar and thought
he was living high. Most summers, Pop bunkered. He
was captain of the *Amagansett* before me. And he did a
good deal of codfishing in the fall. He usually handlined off the beach or set small trawls. We lived on salt
cod in the winter — that and samp. During the cod run,
our ham and eggs tasted like fish. We salted and dried
our cod out in the pightle — what they call the back
yard now — and the stock ate the scraps. One hog we
slaughtered, you couldn't tell the meat from fresh cod.
Samp is a kind of porridge made out of hulled corn
cooked up with dried beans and salt pork. The white
men got it from the Indians. Our Sunday dinner was
always samp and pie and a big pitcher of milk. The reason was samp was one thing that could be cooked the
day before. We didn't break the Sabbath on any ac-

count, even to cook. That was one day when the whales were safe. The 'Gansett beach could be alive with them, but if 'twas Sunday, Pop wouldn't do no more than look. He was a good, God-fearing man. I've seen him some riled, but I never heard him profane. The worst he'd ever come out with was 'cod dum.'

"I can see Pop still, as plain as day, walking the beach or sitting on the stern sheets of a whaleboat, in his old sealskin cap and his old pea jacket that he'd patched himself in a hundred different colors, and his beard tucked in his vest, and his white hair down to his shoulders and blowing in the breeze. He was a big man, as big and strong as me. When he sung out, somebody jumped. It was the same at home or afloat. He was the captain. Mother and us boys and my sister Rosa, who's dead now — we were the crew. I guess Mother was first mate. They saw to it together that the morning sun never shone on any of us in bed. I was doing a boy's work by the time I was five, and a man's work at ten. All of our fun was work. If we wanted to go swimming, we had to take along a clam rake. The place we went to for a picnic was a cranberry bog or a blackberry patch. Pop was stern and he hated idleness, but I never knew him mean. When there was a compliment due, he gave it. He had his own ideas and he was generally right. The first time I ever saw New York City was in 1885, when Pop took me in to Fulton Market with him to sell some whalebone and oil. We stayed at the United States Hotel, on Pearl

Street, and I remember the dressed-up people in the lobby staring at those seven-foot slabs of bone that we had under our arms for samples. Pop stared right back. Anybody didn't like the way he traveled could look the other way. He was one man that wouldn't mimic.

"All I ever wanted was to do things the way my father did, and as good. He taught me just about everything I was able to learn. I had pretty slim schooling after the age of ten. Never went when it interfered with fishing or farming. Until I was fourteen, though, I'd sometimes go back to school in the middle of winter if there was nothing else doing. As soon as I could handle my hands, Pop had me sewing a good sailmaker's herringbone stitch. I mended my clothes and I pieced quilts. The best quilt I made is still in use. There were a good many wrecks in those days. Every so often, a coasting vessel would get in trouble on the bar a quarter mile off here, or on the rocks this side of Montauk Point. Salvage meant a lot to us. After a storm, you could find whatever you needed on the beach. The *George Appold*, a freighter out of Providence and bound for Newport News, is one wreck I remember. Pop and I helped bring the crew off. She went down with a load of calico and copper-toed work shoes in 1889. The quilt I still use is mostly brown-and-white calico from the *George Appold*. Another wreck, in 1890, was the *Elsie Fay*. She carried coconuts. I never cared much for coconut anything after the *Elsie Fay* went down. A good while later, in the winter of 1922, the *Madonna* foundered. She was carrying nothing but liquor. Just about everybody risked pneumonia in the surf that day.

"Pop learned to pull teeth on his voyages, and for some years he was the closest thing to a dentist we had in 'Gansett. He even pulled his own. I can see him twisting and scolding now. He taught me that trade, too. Some thing else I learned from him was how to make a lop fence. You never hear about lop fences any more. They're out of date, like everything else. I understand they never were made anywhere in the world except here on the East End and in some parts of England. The way we did it was this. We picked out a row of young trees in the right place, cut each trunk halfway through about two or three feet from the ground, and then pulled the trees over. The upright part made the post, and the rest of the tree was the bar. It didn't kill the tree, so it kept on growing, but on the horizontal. There never was a better fence to keep cattle out of a wood lot, or one that needed less mending. Over in the Northwest Woods, between here and Sag Harbor, there are still a few lop fences left. They're as old as I am and still going just as strong.

"I learned the most from Pop down on the beach. When I was five, he put me in the surf and told me to come ashore. That's the way all us boys learned to swim. A little later, he began to teach me how to handle an oar, and then how to throw a harpoon. I practiced darting with a wagon stake that was about the heft of a whale iron. That and launching a boat in the surf are two things you can't pick up from a book. You've got to absorb them when you're young. The only grown man I ever knew who got hold of the surf quick was a fellow from Connecticut, a codfisherman. He married a 'Gansett girl, and a brother of hers who had been around surf a lot helped him. To be a surfman and do business right, you've got to know when you can get off and when you can't, and you've got to have oarsmen who have confidence in you. If there's a wind sea — a lot of chop — and the surf is breaking much over eight or nine feet, my advice is stay ashore. You can get off in a heavy sea if it's a ground swell and steady. There is generally three heavy seas and then will come a slatch — two or three smaller seas behind them. You follow as near as you dare after a heavy sea, and if it's smooth behind, let her go. The crew's confidence in the judgment of the boat header, the man at the tiller, is important. And they've got to have discipline. They're rowing, so they're all facing aft. They don't know what's ahead. The boat header is the only one can see, and he gives the orders accordingly. Pop was always boat header when we whaled. Oh, I can hear him now. 'Shove her in!' he'd sing out, and we'd shove her in and each grab an oar. Then 'Pull ahead! Hold water! Stern! Pull ahead!' — and we'd be off and clear.

"That's the one big difference between shore whaling

and deep-sea whaling — the surf. In deep-sea whaling, you launch the whaleboat from the ship. When you go off the beach, you've got the surf to contend with. Otherwise, the two are the same, or were. The whaleboat is the same, the tools are the same, and the methods are the same. I've got my father's whaleboat and all our old gear put away in my daughter's barn. I like to go over there sometimes and just sit down for a while. Pop's boat was built in New London in 1877, when they still knew how, and she's regulation size. She's twenty-eight feet long, six feet wide at the center thwart, and sharp at both ends, with oak ribs and half-inch cedar planks. She's big but light — lighter than some dories. You want a whaleboat that will stand some weather and hold up when you make fast to a whale, but you don't want one so heavy you can't get her off the beach in a hurry. The regulation crew is six, counting all hands. Going off and up till you fasten, every man except the boat header pulls an oar. The boat header steers. On a whaleboat, his tiller a twenty-eight-foot oar. The harpooner is called boat steerer, but he don't steer till after you're fast. He pulls the forward oar, a little fourteen-footer, till you're right on the whale. Then the boat header sings out 'Give it to him!' and the boat steerer ships his oar, gets up his iron, and darts it quick as he can. He's got a second harpoon handy, and he'll hurl it if there's time or need. Soon as he makes fast, he moves aft to take over the steering oar and to tend the towline. Our towline was generally a hundred fathom. It's fixed to the harpoon shank and threaded through a chock in the bow. It runs into a tub about midship, where it's coiled so it won't foul, and then on aft to an upright post — what we call the loggerhead — in the stern. The boat header looks after the line, taking a hitch around the loggerhead, till the boat steerer relieves him. Then the boat header goes forward to kill the whale. He's got two lances there, and he'll throw both. A good man, like Pop, could dart a lance fifty or sixty feet and sink five feet of iron into the whale.

"There's some difference between a harpoon and a lance. People talk as if the harpooner does the killing. He don't. He just makes fast. That's all a harpoon is made for. We used an eleven-foot harpoon — eight foot of hickory shaft and a three-foot iron shank, tempered so it could bend double and not break. The way a harpoon works is this. There is an iron pin that goes through the center of the barbed head to make a hinge and fix it to the shank. Another pin, made of soft wood, holds the head in line with the shaft till it's into the blubber. When the whale sounds, that wooden pin snaps and the head toggles around on the iron pin at a right angle to the rest of the iron. It can't pull out, so you're fast as long as the line holds and the boat don't get stove. A lance is a spear. It's got a ten-foot shaft and a five-foot shank and a razor-edged head. I've seen my father shave with his lance. The other men in the boat mainly just row, but by golly, they earn their pasage. When I went off with Pop, I pulled leading oar, just forward of the boat header. Here in town, though, nobody knew as much as I did about whaling. I generally went boat header then.

"The only whale we ever hunted was the right whale. Finbacks were common, but we didn't try for them. The reason was they're too fast, they don't make much oil, and their bone is short and brittle. Any 'Gansett boy could tell a right whale from a finback just by watching the spout. A whale comes up to breathe and blow every twenty minutes or so. The air he lets out makes the spout. The right whale has two blowholes in the tip of his head, so he'll send up a crotched spout, maybe eight feet high. A finback spouts a single stream. He blows quicker than the right whale and he blows higher. Another way to tell is to watch a whale round out his bilge to go down. The right whale will bring his flukes out of water, but all you'll see of a finback when he rounds to sound is the fin on the afterpart of his bilge.

"The right whale got his name from the old whalemen because he was the right one for oil and bone, especially bone. Whalebone — baleen, to give it its proper name — isn't really bone. Instead of teeth, most whales have a row of long, flat, black, hairy slabs of something like horn set close together in both sides of the upper jaw. That's baleen. A whale lives on a tiny little animal, no bigger than a bug, called brit. When he feeds, he throws back his lips and the brit floats in. The baleen hair acts like a sieve. It lets the water out, but it holds the brit. I've seen slabs of whalebone fourteen feet long and it comes longer than that. I remember Pop telling of some he got on his voyages that measured nineteen feet. There could be close to three thousand pounds of baleen alone in a whale with bone that long. Toward the end of whaling, baleen is what mainly interested us. It generally brought around four dollars a pound. Don't let anybody tell you the whale couldn't swallow Jonah. I remember one we pulled up to. He had his mouth open and his lips laid off. He was feeding. We came up fast, and I just happened to cast my eye around and I looked right down his throat. It must have been fourteen feet deep, and better than a third as wide. I kept pulling, but my blood started to circulate."

Altogether, Edwards estimates, he took part in some thirty chases. Most of his fifteen successful hunts occurred in the eighteen-eighties and nineties. He went off for the first time on a raw and windy day in March, 1887. He was then fifteen and a half. "I was young to whale," he says, "but my father decided I was ready. I was big for my age, almost full-grown, and I pulled an oar as good as a man. He figured I'd watched enough chases and heard enough talk to know. I agreed with him. My recollection is that the weft went out in the forenoon. What we called the weft was an old Ameri-

can flag. It was raised for a signal on a rooftop near the
beach when a whale was sighted. Soon as we'd see the
weft, everybody would sing out 'Whale off!' and make
for the beach. Three boats rallied for the hunt that day,
every one headed by an Edwards. My Uncle Jonathan
headed one, with David Barnes for boat steerer. Another was headed by my Uncle Charles, who was in his
sixties then, with Charles Mulford going boat steerer.
I went with Pop as leading oar, and my Uncle Gabe
Edwards was his boat steerer. Uncle Gabe was as rank
as Pop — ranker, if anything. Oh, he was callous. Nothing
fazed him.

"The whale was laying to the east, about a mile and a
half offshore, when we shoved in. He breached three
times and sounded. We sprung ahead, aiming to get to
him by the next rising, and, pulling hard, with Pop nag-
ging us, we just made it. Pop sung out 'Give it to him,
Gabe!' and Uncle Gabe got fast, right in the back of the
neck, with all his might and main, and his teeth set.
Then Uncle Jonathan come up, and David Barnes put
both his irons in. Pop shifted with Uncle Gabe, but before he could dart his lance, the whale went into his
flurry, head out of water and running in circles. Running
like that meant he was liable to sink. About that moment, Uncle Charles come up, and Charles Mulford
darted. The lances shot right across the whale's nose,
and that last iron riled him. He lifted his nose right
through the middle of their boat. I guess my eyes were

popping out of my head. She rolled over, bottom up, and all hands went in the air — all except Uncle Charles. He was an old man, but he scrambled like a monkey, rolling right over with the boat and ending up sitting astraddle of her keel. There wasn't a drop of water on him. The whale was dead by then. Pop and Uncle Jonathan had lanced him plenty. We began to get the men out of the water. Charles Mulford was the last to come up. He'd gone deep and he come up pale. While he was down there, he told us later, he saw something close by and he put out a hand to shove it away. He shoved, but it didn't budge. Turned out to be the whale's mouth. That whale was a big one, a bull, mostly black but with some white on him. Took us a good while rowing and towing to get him ashore.

"A good many of the whales we raised in those days were that limber. There's one I remember come along around Easter in 1894. Pop had Charles Mulford for boat steerer, and my brother Dave, who was home from medical school for the holiday, was pulling his leading oar. I went off as boat steerer for my Uncle Jess Edwards. Charles Mulford got fast with both irons without much trouble. That's when the fun began. Instead of turning to fight and giving Pop a chance to sicken him quick, the whale settled right down to run. He headed for East Hampton with Pop and them in tow, and then he headed back to 'Ganset, and then he dodged around and made for East Hampton again. He gave them a regular sleigh ride. I guess he hit twenty-five miles an hour. He was some fast whale, and he never slackened. He had them in tow, bow all out of water and the stern sheets near awash, from morning till mid-afternoon. The rest of us couldn't do anything but just lay around and watch while three and a half hours went by. Toward the end, he cut all of a sudden right across our bow. Without waiting for Uncle Jess to call me up — I shouldn't have done it, but I did — I peaked my oar and got around and threw my harpoon. The whale was rounding to go down, and I missed. My iron went about a foot under his small. I never got another chance, but Pop had him at the next rising. He must have lanced him seventy-five times without letting go of the pole. Dave told me afterward that from where he sat aft, all he could see through the spray of thick blood was the top of Pop's head. The whale went into his flurry soon after, and we gave some cheer when he was dead. Charles Mulford did more than yell. He hopped right out and danced a jig on the whale's back.

"Pop got his last whale in 1907, on George Washington's Birthday, when he was seventy-seven years of age. He whaled after that, but he never fastened again. Uncle Gabe was his boat steerer that day, and there were four boats went off — three from 'Gansett and one from East Hampton. I headed the East Hampton boat, with Felix Dominy, who owned her, as boat steerer. We got the first chance — the whale broke water three boat

lengths ahead of us. But when I sung out 'Spring ahead!'
Charles Baker pulled so hard and quick his oar broke.
That put us out. I minded some, but I'd really hoped the
chance would fall to Pop. He hadn't had a whale in a
good while, and he wanted one. Next rising, Uncle
Gabe got fast. Then Pop shifted with him and lanced
the whale as pretty as you please, and 'twas soon over.
That whale wasn't as limber as some, but she was a
good-sized cow. She's the whale they've got in the Museum of Natural History, in New York. Roy Chapman
Andrews was just starting in at the Museum back then,
and my father's last whale was his first job. The Museum heard about that whale somehow, and they sent
him out here to buy her from us. My father figured we
did all right. We got a hundred dollars for the skeleton
and five per cent over the market for the baleen, and we
kept the blubber. I think it made around two thousand
gallons of oil.

"Whaling began to fall off after that chase. The last
whale I, or anybody, got didn't amount to much. 'Twas
only a calf and couldn't have measured over twenty feet.
The old cow that was with him got away. We were rusty
by that time — hadn't been off in three or four years —
and then, toward twilight, a squall come up. Started in
to blow feathers. We were twelve miles offshore when
we had to let the old cow go. As 'twas, it took fifteen
hours of rowing and towing to get the baby ashore. He
didn't make but about thirty gallons of oil, and we never

sold a drop. Nobody cared to buy. All we really got out of that rally was old times' sake."

The right whale, though rare, is not yet wholly extinct. They are still observed from time to time along the eastern Long Island coast. One, a fifty foot cow, turned up just off East Hampton not long after I first met Mr. Edwards. She was raised toward noon by the caretaker of the village bathing pavilion, William Talmage. Talmage is a retired whaler, a robust man of eighty, and he at once telephoned Edwards, who is one of his closest friends. Edwards joined him on the beach a few minutes later. The whale had sounded just as he drove up, and Talmage pointed out where he thought she would be at her next rising. She came up there, blowing lazily, in deep water less than a mile beyond the bar. The two old men stood just off the road on the soft, frosty sand and watched her in silence until she rounded to go down. Then Talmage cleared his throat. "Good-sized," he remarked. "Yes, yes," Edwards said, and turned back to his car.